A History of the 20th Century World
General Editor: C. P. Hill

Russia and
Eastern

D0537575

P. D. Allan
Deputy Head, Whitmore High School, Harrow

Edward Arnold

© P. D. Allan 1983

First published 1983
by Edward Arnold (Publishers) Ltd.
41 Bedford Square, London WC1B 3DQ

British Library Cataloguing in Publication Data
Allan, P.D.
  Russia and Eastern Europe.—(A history of the
  20th century world)
  1. Europe, Eastern—History—20th century
  I. Title   II. Series
  947   DK246

ISBN 0-7131-0680-8

Set by Colset Private Limited, Singapore
Printed in Great Britain by Thomson Litho Ltd, East Kilbride, Scotland

General Editor's Introduction

The broad purpose of this series of six books is to offer a brief, clear and accurate historical background to the main political problems of the contemporary world, and to do so at a standard within the grasp of pupils taking GCE O-level courses in 20th century world history. The difficulties of studying recent world history are obvious enough. Pupils can easily be swamped by detail and by the variety and unfamiliarity of its background — or bored and misled by generalisations. We have tried to avoid this state of affairs by the plan of the series. This puts at the centre a 'core' book providing a narrative of the main international developments of the years since the end of the First World War, and incorporating a fair measure of elementary analysis appropriate to the age of its readers; and links to it five 'area' books dealing respectively with Asia and Australasia, Britain and Western Europe, the Americas, the USSR and Eastern Europe, and Africa and the Middle East. We hope that this scheme, which fits well with current examination syllabuses, will enable pupils to acquire a sound grasp of the most important international events and also to study in rather fuller detail one or two regions of the world. Each book contains maps, diagrams and illustrations, as well as a glossary, list of commonly used abbreviations, booklist, and detailed index. A system of cross-referencing will help students to relate developments in one area to the main progression of world events.*

Those who read these books and use them as a means of study will shortly be citizens of Britain and of the world. In common with young citizens of other lands they will have to help to solve the problems which are emerging from recent world history. Publisher, editor and authors alike believe that there is only limited point in studying the contents of these books merely in order to achieve good grades in examinations. For recent world history is the essential foundation of some understanding of world citizenship. Fully to justify itself, it must help to enlighten the reflections, and stimulate the political actions, of the citizens of the future. We hope most sincerely that the series will make some contribution to these ends.

C. P. Hill

* The system of cross-referencing is as follows:

CORE	= *International Affairs* by E. G. Rayner
AA	= *Asia and Australasia* by J. K. G. Taylor
BWE	= *Britain and Western Europe* by R. D. H. Seaman
REE	= *Russia and Eastern Europe* by P. D. Allan
TA	= *The Americas* by A. B. Lancaster
AME	= *Africa and the Middle East* by J. K. G. Taylor and J. A. Kohler

Author's Introduction

The Union of Soviet Socialist Republics is today a world super-power, its military and industrial might matched only by the USA. The decisions of Russia's leaders are clearly supreme in the satellite states of Eastern Europe; and they are often noted with concern in lands far beyond the boundaries of the Soviet Union. Russia was the first, and for nearly thirty years the only, Communist state. The establishment of the Soviet Union added an ideological dimension to international relations: today the hostility between Communist and non-Communist worlds plays a major part in international tension. A knowledge of the recent history of Russia is essential to an understanding of the 20th century.

The greater part of this book deals with Russia since 1900. At that time Russia, although a major power, was in many ways a backward nation. She had limited industry and the vast majority of her people were peasant farmers. The country was ruled by an emperor, Tsar Nicholas II, who had unlimited power but limited capabilities. In 1917, amid Russian defeats in the First World War, he was removed. Within a few months a small group of dedicated revolutionaries had seized power. Their organization, the Communist Party, has ruled Russia ever since and has made the land into the industrial and military giant of today.

This book considers how and why the Communists came to power; describes the careers, policies and achievements of the leaders since 1917, notably of Lenin, Stalin and Khrushchev; and assesses the effects of their rule upon the Russian people. It attempts to go beyond events, to look at the issues involved and to present the many problems and factors which confronted the policy-makers; and so to give the reader some understanding of the reasons for the decisions taken. The ideas of Karl Marx, upon whose writings Russian communism is supposed to be based, are explained. As the story of Communist rule unfolds, reference is made to these ideas and to the extent to which they affected the policies actually carried out. It is an astounding story of the transformation of a huge country within two generations. Yet within it there is also continuity. For Communist Russia in the last quarter of the 20th century maintains many traditions from Tsarist days — most notably strong central government, very limited freedom for the people, rigid control of ideas, and a vast empire.

Nearly all the countries of Eastern Europe are very closely linked to, even dominated by, the USSR; the presence of the victorious Red Army at the end of the Second World War led easily to the establishment of Communist governments there. The period covered by the book begins with Eastern Europe emerging from the domination of the German, Austro-Hungarian, Russian and Turkish Empires at the end of the First World War. It traces the establishment of independent nation-states, and their individual histories before they fell under the control of Hitler's Germany and later of Stalin's Russia. Their apparent political and ideological uniformity conceals interesting individual developments, developments over which the rulers in Moscow have kept a close watch. The book describes the escape of Tito's Yugoslavia from Stalin's hold; the Russian-led invasions of Hungary (1956) and Czechoslovakia (1968); and the troubles in Poland (1980–2).

P. D. Allan

Contents

Part I   Russia 1905–45   1

1   **Russia in the Early 20th Century**   1
    (1) Agriculture and Industry   1
    (2) Government and Opposition   4
    (3) War with Japan and the Revolution of 1905   8
    (4) The October Manifesto and the Dumas   11

2   **World War and the Two Revolutions of 1917**   12
    (1) The War of 1914–18   12
    (2) The February Revolution (1917) and the Provisional Government 14
    (3) The Return of Lenin and the 'April Theses'   16
    (4) The Rule of Kerensky   17
    (5) The October Revolution (1917) and the Bolshevik Seizure of Power 20

3   **The Establishment and Survival of the Communist State: Russia,
    1917–24**   23
    (1) Bolshevik Dictatorship   23
    (2) The Treaty of Brest-Litovsk (1918)   27
    (3) The Civil War and Foreign Intervention, 1918–21   27
    (4) War Communism and Political Control   32
    (5) The New Economic Policy of 1921   33
    (6) The USSR and its Government   35
    (7) The Bolsheviks and Europe after 1917   37
    (8) The last years of Lenin, and an Assessment   38

4   **Stalin's Russia (I) — The Transformation of a Country**   42
    (1) The Struggle for the Leadership and the Triumph of Stalin   42
    (2) The Soviet Economy and the Future   45
    (3) The Collectivization of Agriculture   49
    (4) Industry and Labour   51

5   **Stalin's Russia (II)**   54
    (1) Education, the Family, and the Arts   54
    (2) The Purges, the Show Trials, and the 1936 Constitution   56
    (3) The 1930s — Some Conclusions   59

6   **Stalin's Russia (III)**   61
    (1) Foreign Affairs, 1924–33   61

(2) The Soviet Union and Nazi Germany, 1933–41   62
(3) The War Comes to Russia — 1941   64
(4) The Battle for Stalingrad and the Russian Triumph, 1942–45   68
(5) Wartime Diplomacy   70

Part II   Eastern Europe Between the Wars   72

7   Eastern Europe 1918–39   72
(1) The Legacy of the First World War   72
(2) The Baltic Republics   77
(3) Poland   78
(4) Hungary   80
(5) Romania   81
(6) Bulgaria   83
(7) Yugoslavia   84
(8) Albania   85
(9) Czechoslovakia   86

Part III   Russia since 1945   89

8   Stalin's Russia (IV)   89
(1) The Cold War   89
(2) Russia at Home, 1945–53: Recovery, Expansion and Repression   92
(3) Stalin — an Assessment   95

9   Soviet Russia Under Khrushchev   97
(1) De-Stalinization and the Secret Speech of 1956   97
(2) Khrushchev's Rise to Supremacy   101
(3) Agriculture, Industry and Living Standards   101
(4) Foreign Policy, 1953–64   105
(5) Khrushchev's Fall   109

10   Soviet Russia since 1964   110
(1) Agriculture and Industry   111
(2) Stalinism, the Dissidents, and Minority Groups   113
(3) Soviet Foreign Policy since 1964   114
(4) The USSR in 1981   117

Part IV   Eastern Europe since 1945   119

11   Eastern Europe since the Second World War   119
(1) The Soviet Take-over and Communist Policy   119
(2) East Germany   124
(3) Poland   125
(4) Hungary   129
(5) Romania   132
(6) Bulgaria   134
(7) Yugoslavia   135
(8) Albania   138
(9) Czechoslovakia   139

Guide to abbreviations used in *A History of the 20th Century World*

Many abbreviations have come into everyday political use during the 20th century. The list below provides the meanings of some which are widely used (note that, for several, translation into English involves a change of the initial letter). Others, less commonly used, will be explained in the text or index of the series book(s) in which they appear.

ANZUK	Anzuk Pact (of Australia, New Zealand and UK, 1971)
ANZUS	Anzus Pact (of Australia, New Zealand and USA, 1951)
ASEAN	Association of South-East Asian Nations (1967)
BDR	Bundesrepublik Deutschland (German Federal Republic, i.e. West Germany; also GFR)
BENELUX	originally (1947) the Customs Union of Belgium, the Netherlands and Luxemburg
CCP	Chinese Communist Party
CENTO	Central Treaty Organization
CIA	Central Intelligence Agency (USA)
COMECON	Council for Mutual Economic Assistance (1949)
COMINFORM	Communist International 'Information bureau' (from 1947)
COMINTERN	Communist International (1919–43)
CPSU	Communist Party of the Soviet Union
DDR	Deutsche Demokratische Republik (German Democratic Republic, i.e., East Germany; also GDR)
ECSC	European Coal and Steel Community
EDC	European Defence Community
EEC	European Economic Community (known at first as the Common Market)
EFTA	European Free Trade Association
ENOSIS	The movement for the Union of Greece with Cyprus
EURATOM	European Atomic Energy Community
FAO	Food and Agriculture Organization (of UN)
FBI	Federal Bureau of Investigation (USA)
FLN	Front de la Libération Nationale (Algerian National Liberation Front)
FNLA	The National Front (Angola)
GATT	General Agreement on Tariffs and Trade
GDR	German Democratic Republic (East Germany; also DDR)
GFR	German Federal Republic (West Germany; also BRD)
GNP	Gross National Product
ICBM	Inter-Continental Ballistic Missile
ILO	International Labour Organization
IMF	International Monetary Fund
IRA	Irish Republican Army
IRBM	Intermediate Range Ballistic Missile
KGB	Committee of State Security (Soviet Russia)
KKK	Ku-Klux-Klan (USA)

KMT	Kuomintang (China)
KPD	Kommunistische Partei Deutschlands (German Communist Party)
LAFTA	Latin American Free Trade Association
MPLA	Popular Movement for the Liberation of Angola
MRP	Mouvement Républicain Populaire
NAACP	National Association for the Advancement of Colored People
NATO	North Atlantic Treaty Organization
NAZI	from Nationalsozialistische Deutsche Arbeiterpartei (NSDAP, the National Socialist Party)
NEP	New Economic Policy (Soviet Russia)
NLF	National Liberation Front (South Vietnam, from 1960)
OAS	(1) Organization of American States
	(2) Organization of the Secret Army (France and Algeria)
OAU	Organization of African Unity
OECD	Organization for Economic Cooperation and Development
OEEC	Organization for European Economic Cooperation
OPEC	Organization of Petroleum Exporting Countries
PLO	Palestine Liberation Organization
POLITBURO	The principal committee of the government in Communist countries
SA	Sturmabteilung (in Nazi Germany — 'Brown shirts')
SALT	Strategic Arms Limitation Talks
SAM	Surface-to-air Missile
SCAP	Supreme Commander for the Allied Powers (General MacArthur in Japan after 1945)
SDP	Social Democratic Party (Germany; see SPD)
SEATO	South-East Asia Treaty Organization
SHAPE	Supreme Headquarters, Allied Powers, Europe
SPD	Sozialdemokratische Partei Deutschlands (Germany; see SDP)
SS	Schutzstaffel (in Nazi Germany — 'Black shirts')
SWAPO	South-West Africa People's Organization (Namibia)
TUC	Trades Union Congress
TVA	Tennessee Valley Authority (USA)
UAE	United Arab Emirates
UAR	United Arab Republic (1958–71)
UDI	Unilateral Declaration of Independence
UN/UNO	United Nations/Organization
UNCTAD	United Nations Conference on Trade and Development
UNESCO	United Nations Educational, Scientific and Cultural Organization
UNICEF	United Nations Children's Emergency Fund
UNITA	National Union for Total Independence (Angola)
UNRRA	United Nations Relief and Rehabilitation Organization
UNRWA	United Nations Relief and Works Agency
USA	United States of America
USSR	Union of Soviet Socialist Republics
VC	Vietcong
WEU	Western European Union
WHO	World Health Organization

Acknowledgements

The Author's and Publishers' thanks are due to the following for permission to reproduce copyright photographs:

Novosti Press Agency: pp 3, 6, 7, 20, 25, 39, 54, 70, 102, 105, 110, 111, 116;
Popperfoto: 5, 16, 18, 43, 57, 65, 79, 82, 94, 99, 128, 130;
BBC Hulton Picture Library: pp 9, 10t, 12, 13, 75;
Imperial War Museum: pp 10b, 19, 135;
John Frost Newspaper Archive: pp 29, 63;
The School of Slavonic Studies: p 30;
Snark: p 35;
TUC Photograph Library: pp 46, 90b;
Hans Tasiemka Archive/Daily Express: pp 90t, 121;
Camera Press: p 133;
John Hillelson Agency Ltd/Magnum: p 140.

Maps, Diagrams and Tables

Russia in the early 20th century   2
The Treaty of Brest-Litovsk, 1918   26
The Civil War and foreign intervention   28
Grain production and state purchase   50
Russia under attack, 1941-3   66
A comparison of Eastern Europe before and after the First World War   73
Eastern Europe between the wars   74
The destruction of Eastern European independence, 1938-9   76
Yugoslavia   84
Eastern Europe after 1945   120

Part I
Russia 1905–45

1

Russia in the Early 20th Century

Tsar Nicholas II, Tsar of Russia from 1894, inherited with the imperial crown responsibility for an empire that occupied one-sixth of the land surface of the world. Stretching from Poland in the west to the Pacific Ocean in the east, from the Arctic Circle in the north to the Black Sea in the south, it was an area of considerable diversity in climate and landscape, and in the variety of peoples who attempted to make a living within it. The vast majority of the inhabitants were peasant farmers, living in scattered village communities.

(1) Agriculture and Industry

Agriculture
By Western standards Russian agriculture was backward. The peasants farmed with simple hand tools, used wooden ploughs, and had but a few animals to speed up the process. Most peasants had been serfs until 1861. They had worked on their master's land as his private possessions, with no rights to move away or even to marry without his permission. They could be bought or sold and were, on occasion, even gambled away at the card table. Tsar Alexander II had freed the serfs in 1861, yet their lot had not greatly improved. The village community (or *mir*) had been given land, but it had to be paid for over 49 years. This, together with the pressure of an increasing population on the land available, meant that great hardship continued for the majority. Their day-to-day concern with mere survival contrasted sharply with the wealth, education, and life-style of the tiny minority of rich landowners and nobles, and with the royal household in the capital, St Petersburg.

Industrial development
Russia's potential as an industrial nation was beginning to be realized by the late 19th century. Her huge mineral resources of coal and iron in the

Donets Basin were first exploited in the 1860s, and from the 1890s the pace of industrial development quickened. Much financial investment came from France, with whom Russia signed an alliance in 1894. Production rose rapidly: for example, coal production went up from 5·9 million tons in 1890 to 35·4 million in 1913; pig iron production rose from 890 000 tons to 4·1 million over the same period. Railway building proceeded apace: by 1913 Russia had 70 600 kilometres of track, the most famous line being the Trans-Siberian, linking European Russia with Vladivostock in the far east.

Russia in the early 20th century; Russia occupied about a sixth of the total land surface of the world

Poverty in Russia in the early twentieth century

Large industrial towns grew, especially in western Russia. By 1911 there were about one million mine workers, three million factory workers and 800 000 railwaymen out of a total population of 160 million. They had far greater significance than their numbers alone might suggest, for they were not part of the traditional peasant society which instinctively respected authority as represented by the Church and the nobility. They lived and worked alongside one another and could therefore be more easily organized than the peasantry into taking trade union or political action to improve their lives. As a group they were highly discontented. The workers in Russia's industrial revolution suffered the same hardships that their counterparts in western Europe and America had experienced, or were living under at that time. Hours were extremely long, pay was very low, and conditions were brutal. Little regard was shown for the health or safety of the work force. Women and children were employed as cheap labour wherever possible. The towns in which they lived were little better. Living quarters were overcrowded and barrack-like, lacking the basic amenities and sanitation to preserve life, let alone self-respect. Attempts by workers to form trade unions were usually thwarted by the owners and by the government, who saw in workers' organizations a threat to their profits or a possible cover for political activity of a dangerous kind.

Workers' conditions

(2) Government and Opposition

The power of
the Tsar

The political, social and economic problems accompanying Russia's development in the 20th century would have tested any system of government. The government which had to face them was in no way fit for the task, for Russia was an autocracy, that is, the Tsar had absolute power. The government of Russia was his government, the ministers were appointed by him and responsible only to him: they could be dismissed when he saw fit. He could take their advice if he wished, but decisions were his to make, not theirs. There was no Parliament to limit his power. He was answerable only to God. As Alexander III had written:

> The voice of God orders us to stand firm at the helm of government . . . with faith in the strength and truth of the autocratic power, which we are called to strengthen and preserve, for the good of the people, from every kind of encroachment.

The Tsar was supported by the army, the police, a vast bureaucracy of officials and the Russian Orthodox Church. The last had considerable influence over the mass of the people and preached acceptance of the existing social order as the will of God. Russians did not expect to find heaven on earth — the greatest rewards would come in after-life.

Alexander II, the liberator of the serfs, had been blown to pieces by a terrorist's bomb in 1881. His successor, Alexander III (1881–94), had responded by clamping down on all opposition to the existing political and social system. His secret police force was much used; so was the practice of exiling dangerous political opponents to Siberia. He also adopted a policy of

'Russification'

'Russification', which aimed at removing the local privileges, languages, and religions of the subject nationalities within the empire. The Russians and their language were to dominate, and the true religion of the Russian Orthodox Church was to be spread wherever possible. Since over half the population was not Russian, this was rather foolish. Many of the peoples, whose language and culture were threatened, became supporters of the revolutionaries who aimed to bring down Tsardom altogether.

In addition, persecution of the Jews was stepped up. There were already considerable restrictions on their rights to settle where they wished, to own land, and to be educated; and the Tsarist government often whipped up anti-Jewish feeling, encouraging violent attacks on Jewish life and property. These were known as pogroms. Not surprisingly many Jews were later found in the ranks of the revolutionaries.

Nicholas and
Alexandra

Nicholas II (1894–1917) continued the policies of his father, determined to preserve the Russia he knew, and the power that he held, saying 'I shall uphold the principle of autocracy as firmly and undeviatingly as did my late father'. Russia needed a man with flair and drive as Tsar. She had instead a well-meaning family man with a limited imagination; a monarch who would have managed a country estate well, but could not cope with the problems of a changing empire. His wife, the Tsarina Alexandra, reinforced his own prejudices against change and against sharing his power with his people.

Opposition

Opposition to the government and demand for change came from many different quarters. It was vocal and at times violent. Among the educated noblemen and the growing middle classes of businessmen and professionals

The middle
classes

were many who felt that Russia desperately needed change. She had to progress into the modern world. The best way to achieve this seemed to be the establishment of a form of elected Parliament, which could pass laws to suit the needs of business, bring greater freedom to Russia, and remedy many of the grievances of the Russian people.

Wealth in Russia (the Tsar and Tsarina, Nicholas II and Alexandra)

While supporting the call for more representative government, other groups wanted a complete change, not just in the political system but in the whole social order. They wanted changes that would bring freedom and a distribution of the wealth of the country among the majority of its citizens. They realized there was little likelihood of achieving their aims, or even of getting the government to listen to them. So many were prepared to turn to violence. The revolutionary group which was to have the most significance

The Marxists

for later Russian history was the Russian Social Democratic party founded in 1898. This small party followed the teachings of Karl Marx as set down in his writings *Das Kapital* and *The Communist Manifesto*. Marx maintained that 'the history of all hitherto existing society is the history of class struggles', struggles between those who own the means of production, the land or factories or mines, and those who are forced to work for them. He saw the economic system of a country, and those who owned its wealth, dictating who had the power and so the type of government. A country starts as a feudal state where society is made up of large landowners and landless peasants. Its government is run for and by these landowners (usually with a king and his noblemen taking the decisions). Gradually, commerce and industry begin to dominate; the wealth is now in the hands of factory owners and businessmen who own the capital, that is, the land, factories, and money. These bourgeois (middle-class) 'capitalists' employ industrial workers (otherwise called the proletariat) to work for them and make a profit from their labour. The government of the country changes accordingly, to one in which these capitalists have power.

Karl Marx

According to Marx, the workers would be exploited, working long hours for low pay. Their conditions would get worse and worse until in the end they would combine to overthrow their bosses in a revolution. The workers would take over the means of 'production, distribution, and exchange' (the land and factories, trade, and all the financial institutions) and would abolish private ownership. Their eventual aim was the end of the class system which was based on some people owning the property and others working for them. Instead, farms, factories, and businesses would be run by the workers collectively and the profits would be shared. People would therefore not be working simply to make as much money as they could for themselves, but for the community as a whole. The ultimate ideal was communism where the slogan, 'from each according to his ability, to each according to his need', would apply. Everyone would work as best they could, according to their ability, and people would be paid according to their individual needs, not according to the value of their work. In the long run the country would be managed by elected committees, and the need for a strong central government would wither away. Marx claimed that the latter was only essential in a class-based society, where the central government was a means of keeping the lower orders in their place. During the transition period, strong government (a 'dictatorship of the proletariat') would be needed to carry out the changes, to deal with the former property owners who would fight to regain their former possessions, and to educate the people to the new values that a communist society involved.

Marx wanted:

the forcible overthrow of all existing social conditions. . . . Let the ruling classes tremble at a Communistic revolution. The proletarians have nothing to lose but their chains. They have a world to win. . . . Working men of all countries unite.

He believed that only revolution, not evolution (gradual change), would bring about the sort of society he wished to see because property owners would not willingly give up their power. He also believed that the revolution would be started by the industrial workers, not the peasantry. The latter were too traditional, showed too much respect for their social superiors, and were too difficult to organize. For this reason, the Russian Marxists concentrated their attention on the workers in Russia's growing industrial towns. This was in sharp contrast to the policy of the other main revolutionary group, the Socialist Revolutionaries (otherwise known as Populists or *Narodniks*), who had similar aims to the Marxists, but believed that the revolution would come from the peasant communities — the *mirs*.

Lenin

Among the founders of the Social Democrats in Russia were Georgiy Plekhanov and Vladimir Ilyich Ulyanov (later known as Lenin). Born in 1870, the son of an inspector of schools, Lenin was forcefully introduced to revolutionary ideas when, in 1887, his brother Alexander was executed for his part in an attempt on the life of the Tsar. By the time Lenin reached the University of Kazan to study law he was fully immersed in revolutionary

Lenin aged 22

ideas. He was soon expelled because of his political activities. A brilliant scholar, he was later to qualify by taking external examinations in St Petersburg, and he practised as a lawyer for a short while. His main interests were, however, political. Much of his time was spent, in exile, in Siberia. Alternatively, he was abroad, safe from the activities of the Russian secret police, and free to discuss his ideas with other revolutionaries and to organize the publication of a Marxist newspaper *Iskra* ('The Spark') for circulation in Russia.

Party split 1903   The Communist Party could not meet openly in Russia, and members often met abroad. At the party conference held in London in the summer of 1903 they split on how it should best be organized. Lenin wanted party membership restricted to a hard core of dedicated revolutionaries, rather than let it be open to all sympathizers; and he wanted the party run by a small committee, which would command absolute obedience. Lenin won The Bolsheviks the day and his followers took the name 'Bolsheviks' (or majority) — the others being known as 'Mensheviks' (or minority). Such debates and wrangles seemed wildly unrealistic in 1903 as there seemed little hope of putting their ideas into practice. Yet events were conspiring to alter the situation and to bring the Tsar close to downfall in 1905.

(3) War with Japan and the Revolution of 1905

In 1904 Russian expansion in the Far East, especially in North Korea, had led to Japanese anger and a consequent attack by Japan, who felt her own interests in the area were threatened. Few doubted that the might of Russia would soon crush the 'upstarts' of Japan. Nicholas himself believed the Japanese 'to be little better than monkeys, who could be taught a sharp lesson'. In fact, the initial Japanese successes were never reversed by the Russian armed forces. Even the gamble of sending the Russian Baltic Fleet halfway round the world came to nothing when the Japanese navy sank it at Tsushima Straits in May 1905 in forty-five minutes. The Russian people were shocked and dismayed and they naturally blamed the generals and government for their apparent incompetence.

Bloody Sunday   While the war was in progress discontent mounted among Russia's town dwellers. Prices were rising, wages barely paid for essentials, and people were increasingly unwilling to make the sacrifices demanded of them. On Sunday 22 January 1905, a huge procession marched to the Tsar's Winter Palace in St Petersburg to present a petition to their 'little father'. It was a common belief at the time that the Tsar cared for his people, but that he was surrounded by evil advisers. The marchers were led by Father Gapon, a Russian Orthodox priest, who was also in the pay of the government as a police agent. The Tsar had had notice of the demonstration and of the petition, but had left the capital for the weekend, leaving instructions that order was to be maintained. So the marchers, who came in peace, singing hymns and carrying pictures of the Tsar, were met with a hail of bullets. No one knows exactly how many were killed — it may have been as many as 1000. The day became known as 'Bloody Sunday' and Tsarist Russia was never quite the same again.

The 1905   The workers' discontent, combined with anger at the way the war was
Revolution   being so inefficiently prosecuted against Japan, brought wholesale disorder

Bloody Sunday, 1905

to Russia in the summer of 1905. This took many different forms. Peasant riots in the countryside led to the destruction of property; strikes by industrial workers and professional people, such as bankers and lawyers, culminated in a general strike; the armed forces could not be relied upon to restore order; and in the navy there was a mutiny on board Russia's most modern battleship, the *Potemkin*. The industrial workers in St Petersburg and Moscow, determined to use the occasion to win better conditions and a say in the government, elected councils to organize action against their bosses and the government. These councils became known as Soviets. Many

Trotsky

of the revolutionaries abroad returned to make the most of the situation. Leon Trotsky, a brilliant but arrogant Jewish intellectual, was the most active, and he became very prominent in the St Petersburg Soviet.

Revolutionaries burning and sacking a house, 1905

Trotsky

(4) The October Manifesto and the Dumas

With the situation beyond his control the Tsar had no choice but to make certain concessions. In the October Manifesto of 1905 he agreed to share his power with an elected Russian Parliament, or Duma. This action was sufficient to persuade most people back to work and to restore the loyalty of the armed forces. These were now used to crush the continuing opposition of the Soviets, who wanted more of their demands met and who, anyway, did not trust the Tsar to keep his word.

With order restored, Nicholas soon made it clear that he had no intention of really giving up his power. He declared that:

> the Emperor of All Russia has supreme autocratic power. It is ordained by God himself that this authority should be submitted to, not only out of fear but out of a genuine sense of duty.

This did not bode well for the future, and when the first Duma duly met in 1906 and put a long list of demands for change to the Tsar, he refused to agree to them. Instead he dismissed the delegates and a second election took place. But the Duma which met in 1907 proved just as awkward for the Tsar to handle, and met the same fate as the first. To avoid a further repetition of events, voting for the third Duma was restricted to the wealthy. They elected representatives sympathetic to the Tsar — like him, they had no wish to see Russia drastically altered. The third Duma lasted its full term from 1907 to 1912 and the fourth met from 1912 to 1917.

Few important laws were enacted, although reforms were passed to enable more peasants to buy their land. This was the idea of the Tsar's chief minister, Peter Stolypin, who saw the measures as a way of lessening tension in the countryside.

General distress and defeat in war had resulted in a revolution in 1905. The autocracy had been shaken, but not overthrown. It had been given a chance to put its house in order, to bring in some form of representative government and to introduce measures to lessen the misery of the masses. The chance had not been taken. The point was not lost on many of the opponents of Tsardom. When a second war and further hardship came, the Tsar was not to be given a second chance. 1905 was to prove just a dress rehearsal.

2

World War and the Two Revolutions of 1917

(1) The War of 1914–18

On 26 July 1914 Austria-Hungary declared war on the small Balkan state of Serbia. The Russian armies were duly mobilized to protect Serbia, and within a week the Germans had declared war on Russia and her ally France.

In Russia the declaration of war produced an outburst of patriotism and anti-German feeling so strong that the capital was renamed; the German-sounding Sankt Petersburg was replaced by the Russian Petrograd. Despite the industrial unrest and class divisions which had been evident before the war, Nicholas found a surprisingly united nation behind him. The Russian armies advanced on Germany, invading East Prussia, and the speed of their mobilization somewhat surprised the Germans. But the effectiveness of the Russian army was illusory. The high command relied on weight of numbers — the Russian army was renowned as the 'steamroller' — and on outmoded tactics, such as the use of the bayonet and the cavalry charge, more suited to eighteenth–century warfare. The Germans soon defeated the Russians at Tannenberg and at the Masurian Lakes. The invasion of East Prussia was estimated to have cost the Russians almost a quarter of a million men.

Early defeat

Cossack soldiers in the Caucasus, 1916

Although they had some successes against the Austrians, defeat by the Germans soon led to rout. Most of Poland was lost to Germany in 1915. The German soldiers became sickened by the huge number of casualties they were inflicting. One Russian general remarked, 'The army is drowning in its own blood'.

Success in the modern form of warfare lay with the industrial nations of the world, who were able to mass-produce up-to-date weapons and ammunition and who had an efficient network of road and rail communications. Russian industry simply could not keep pace with demand. By 1915, many of the frontline soldiers were without guns; they had to wait for colleagues to fall so that they could pick up theirs. There were instances of soldiers being issued with only four bullets a day! The transport system was totally inadequate. Most of Russia's railways were in the west and soon fell into enemy hands; lorries were in very short supply and horse transport was often all that remained. Many of the horses had been requisitioned from the peasants, who thus found themselves without animals to help farm the land.

Rasputin

The failures of the war were blamed on the government. There were loud demands from many Russians, including some of the Tsar's close advisers, for a government more representative of the nation. Nicholas refused such a call and his most capable ministers either resigned or were dismissed. The Tsar was most distressed by the military disasters and, in 1915, he decided to assume command of the forces himself, in the hope that this would bring renewed vigour and efficiency to the war effort. This was the autocrat's answer.

Rasputin In his absence at the front Russia was left in the charge of the Tsarina Alexandra and a host of nonentities, many of whom owed their position at court to the influence of Gregori Rasputin. Rasputin, a supposed holy man with special powers, had come to the notice of the royal couple because of his ability to ease the pain of their only son, Alexis. The boy suffered from haemophilia, a disease whereby the blood does not clot if a wound occurs. Rasputin's importance in Russian history lay not in his curative powers, nor in his wild life of drinking and womanizing, but in the fact that his influence extended to the political decisions which governed the country. His advice was undoubtedly harmful to the survival of Tsardom, for he recommended the most reactionary and incompetent people for high places. He certainly helped to bring the reputation of the monarchy to a low ebb, and the nobility and those excluded from power deeply resented his influence. A group of nobles, led by a certain Prince Yusupov, plotted his murder towards the end of 1916. They invited Rasputin to dinner and heavily laced his food and drink with poison. This failed to kill him; nor were bullets fired into him at close range any more successful. Eventually, he was battered with an iron bar, shot again, tied up, and pushed beneath the ice of the river Neva. When his body was recovered some time later the ropes had been broken and his lungs were full of water, suggesting he had still been alive when he was dumped in the river.

(2) The February Revolution (1917) and the Provisional Government

By the early months of 1917 Russia was on the brink of chaos. Less food had been produced than normal because of the need for manpower in the forces and because of the loss of animals to the front line. The breakdown in the transport system meant that the available food often did not reach the towns. The people became increasingly discontented as prices had risen four times as fast as wages since 1914. In Petrograd the Putilov steel workers came out on strike; soon there were 200 000 strikers in the capital. Violence erupted in the streets because of the bread shortages and, by late February, the

Bread riots situation was fast going out of control. The Tsarina seemed unaware of the seriousness of the situation. She wrote to Nicholas that 'The disturbances are created by hoodlums. . . . They do this just to create some excitement'. She relied on troops to keep order, but their loyalty was wavering. They were not willing to fire on unarmed civilians and, without the use of force, order could not be restored.

The President of the Duma telegraphed Nicholas that the capital was falling into chaos and that some drastic change was now vital. Nicholas' response was to dismiss the Duma and to attempt to return to the capital. The Duma ignored the Tsar, and instead chose a 12-man committee to take over the government. Nicholas' journey back to Petrograd ended at Pskov. Railway workers prevented him from going further, and here he was forced to abdicate by members of the Duma. He did so in favour of his brother, the Grand Duke Michael, the young Alexis being too sickly to bear the burden of rule. Under pressure from the Duma the Grand Duke did not accept the crown. The royal family was imprisoned and later in the year transported to Siberia on the orders of the Provisional Government. A revolution had occurred; the last of the Romanovs had fallen, and Russia now became a republic.

The new government of Russia called itself the Provisional Government. It would rule until elections clarified the wishes of the Russian people. For the most part, its middle-class and upper-class members aimed at a form of parliamentary democracy, with basic rights and freedoms guaranteed to the individual. Among its first decrees were those allowing freedom of speech and assembly. The hated Tsarist police and gendarmerie were abolished.

Headed by the liberal nobleman, Prince Lvov, the Provisional Government believed that its primary task was to reorganize the war effort to bring the war to a successful conclusion. When the war was over elections for a Parliament, or Constituent Assembly, could take place and further reforms would follow. High on the list would be land reform. Some of the more radical members of the government wanted a redistribution of the huge landed estates of the nobles.

But the government soon found that its authority was far from total. On the same day as the election of the 12-man Duma Committee, 27 February, a council of elected delegates representing the workers of Petrograd and the soldiers was formed, under the name of the Soviet of Workers' and Soldiers' Deputies. This was heir to the workers' councils, or Soviets, of 1905. Their example was soon followed in other parts of the country. The Soviets generally controlled the economic and military activity of the country, and had the loyalty of the soldiers and workers; so the orders of the Provisional Government were almost impossible to carry out unless the Soviets agreed to them. This was very quickly made clear by the Petrograd Soviet's Order No. 1 to the soldiers in Petrograd, which directed them to elect Soviets among the soldiers. These Soviets were to decide whether to accept the orders of the officers (apart from actual battle orders), to keep control of the weapons, and to carry out the instructions of the Provisional Government only if they did not conflict with the wishes of the Soviet. The latter feared that the army might be used to restore the Tsar. Although Order No. 1 was initially only for Petrograd, it was soon taken up by the army at the front and the traditional discipline of the forces disappeared.

The early Soviets were dominated by Mensheviks and Socialist Revolutionaries. Although their priorities were somewhat different from those of the Provisional Government (for example on land reform), they co-operated with it. They felt that all opponents of the Tsar should work together. Even the Bolsheviks, who had returned to Russia, worked with the government in its first month, since they believed that the establishment of a liberal (bourgeois) democracy was a necessary stage in the Marxist theory of

Marginal notes:
Abdication of Nicholas II

Aims of the Provisional Government

The Soviet

development towards a communist state. They also feared that quarrels among the revolutionaries would allow the Tsar to regain power. They were even prepared to co-operate with a government which continued the war, although they called for peace. But their co-operation lasted only until the return of Lenin.

(3) The Return of Lenin and the 'April Theses'

Lenin's view of the war   Lenin, who had spent the years since 1914 in neutral Switzerland, had very definite views on the war. He was absolutely against it, saying that normal wars had no relevance at all for the workers and soldiers of the countries involved. They were the wars of the ruling classes. What was needed was a continuation of the class struggle. Lenin had written: 'Our slogan must be Civil War.' Before 1914 most European socialist and Marxist parties had been against wars, but once war had been declared in that year, nearly every one had committed itself to a patriotic struggle for national survival. Lenin had nothing but contempt for this conduct. Nor did he believe that it was necessary for Russia in 1917 to go through a stage of liberal democracy before proceeding to a second revolution in which the masses would take power. The Bolsheviks, he said, should be working against the Provisional Government, not with it.

Lenin arriving at the Finland Station in Petrograd, 1917

He had despaired of ever seeing a revolution in his lifetime, especially if the Bolsheviks did not seize the opportunities that were offered, and he was very keen to return to Russia to push out the 'bourgeois democrats' and to further the Marxist cause by a second revolution. He was, however, stuck on the wrong side of Europe and Russia's allies were hardly likely to aid his return in view of his beliefs on war and revolution. Help in fact came from Russia's enemy, Germany. The Germans decided to help Lenin to return to Russia, for they believed that once he arrived he would cause so much trouble for the new Russian government that he would seriously weaken their war effort. If he actually got into power, he was committed to ending the war; so neither way could the Germans lose. A special sealed train was provided for Lenin and a small party of followers; they crossed Germany, and then proceeded via Sweden to Finland. From there they arrived at the Finland Station in Petrograd on 3 April to a tumultuous welcome.

Lenin returns with German help

Lenin had little time for the niceties of welcoming speeches. By the following day he was already lecturing the Bolsheviks on the line to be taken. His ideas were made public as the 'April Theses'. The Bolsheviks should not co-operate with the Provisional Government, for the promises it made were just a bourgeois plot which would keep the middle-classes in power and would do little to improve the lot of the average person. Instead, they should work for the overthrow of the government and of capitalism. The peasants must meanwhile seize the land, and the workers must take over the factories. The power of the Soviets should be built up and so should that of the Bolsheviks within them.

The 'April Theses'

Many party members were shocked at his policy of non-co-operation, yet after a few days of intense argument, Lenin was able to convince them that the opportunities were not to be missed. The slogan 'Peace, Bread and Land' encapsulated the Bolshevik programme. 'Peace' involved an end to the war, but it was peace with the German workers rather than the Kaiser, since it was hoped a German revolution would follow. 'Bread' meant enough food for all, and 'Land' meant that the land should go to the peasants. The last point was not seen as more than a step on the road to socialism; it was a way of gaining mass support and at the same time ridding Russia of its rich landowners.

Promises ('Peace, Bread and Land')

Bolshevik strength was, at this stage, still limited. In April 1917 there were probably 50 000 party members, although this increased to about 240 000 during the summer months as the Provisional Government failed to solve the pressing problems. A large measure of this support was in Petrograd and Moscow, so the Bolshevik Party was able to bring more pressure to bear on events than their numbers might suggest.

(4) The Rule of Kerensky

At this time the individual with the greatest popular following was not Lenin but Alexander Kerensky, a moderate socialist and one of the few people to be a member both of the Provisional Government and of the Petrograd Soviet. A member of the government since its formation, Kerensky was a firm believer in waging a successful war against Germany and in solving Russia's problems in a democratic manner. He became Minister of War in May 1917 and Prime Minister in July. However, his popularity did not extend to the mass of workers and soldiers in Petrograd. Along with 20 000 armed sailors from the nearby Kronstadt naval base, they came out onto the streets demonstrating against the government, and

The 'July Days'

demanding 'All Power to the Soviets'. These mass protests of the 'July Days' caught the Bolsheviks by surprise. They did not know whether to try to quieten the protests down or to harness the mass feeling to destroy the government. Lenin was worried at the possibility of missing a golden opportunity — he was only too aware of the lost chances of 1905 — yet he was also conscious that it was too early for the Bolsheviks. Kerensky still had too much support and if the slogan 'All Power to the Soviets' were implemented that would mean power to the Mensheviks and Social Revolutionaries, not the Bolsheviks who were still in a minority in the Soviets. The Bolsheviks therefore hesitated and Kerensky was quick to seize the initiative. He summoned loyal troops from the front to put down the rioters and to seize Bolshevik headquarters. Lenin fled once again, and remained in Finland until October. Meanwhile, other leaders were arrested. These included Trotsky, who had returned to Russia a month after Lenin and who had joined the Bolsheviks, despite formerly adhering to the Mensheviks. The party, however, was not smashed and lived on.

The summer offensive

Kerensky's quick action seemed to have saved the day. But events elsewhere were undermining his position. A summer offensive had been launched at the end of June, but despite its initial success it was soon repulsed by the Germans. Within a few weeks the Russian armies were again in retreat. Kerensky had been no more able to wage the war successfully than the Tsar, and indeed it was probably beyond anyone to do so by that stage.

Demonstrations in Petrograd during the July Days, 1917

Young Russian women soldiers — part of the 'Battalion of Death' created by the provisional government in 1917

The Bolsheviks had already done much to undermine discipline in the forces. The soldiers now began to desert in huge numbers, sickened by continual defeat and unwilling to fight on in a hopeless situation. In the countryside the peasants began to seize the land without waiting for government reforms, and the soldiers were keen not to miss their share. Russia was once more collapsing into anarchy. Army desertion, peasant disorders, the 'July Days', and the break-up of the old Russian empire, as various nationalities demanded their independence, were all signs of a situation going out of control.

The Kornilov revolt

Many people in the left and centre political parties (the Mensheviks, Liberals, Constitutional Democrats) pinned their hopes on the future elected Constituent Assembly. But many of the more conservative elements began to look to the army to restore order. The new Commander-in-Chief was the popular hero, General Lavr Kornilov. Kerensky wanted him to be ready to deal with any new trouble from the Bolsheviks, but Kornilov decided that the time had come to replace Kerensky with a new dictatorship under himself. Kornilov thought Kerensky too weak and too socialist to be worth protecting. In the last week of August he began to march on the capital. Kerensky's position was desperate and he was forced to call on the support of the left-wing groups, including the Bolsheviks, to save him. The imprisoned Bolshevik leaders were freed and arms were handed over to them. The Petrograd workers and soldiers were ready to fight to stop Kornilov rather than to save Kerensky, but it proved unnecessary. The railway workers again intervened, refusing to bring in supplies or troops for Kornilov, and Bolshevik propaganda and persuasion led to the disintegration of his forces. He was soon arrested.

(5) The October Revolution (1917) and the Bolshevik Seizure of Power

Trotsky and the Red Guards The Kornilov affair had shown the weakness of the Provisional Government. Kerensky and his Menshevik and Socialist Revolutionary allies were discredited. In the following weeks the Bolsheviks gradually gained a majority in the Petrograd and Moscow Soviets. Trotsky became Chairman of the Petrograd Soviet and he now began to develop a plan for seizing power. A Military Revolutionary Committee was established — officially to defend Petrograd against the Germans, as Kerensky was on the point of transferring the capital further east to Moscow, but really to prepare a military take-over by the Bolshevik Red Guards. Trotsky whipped up support among the soldiers and workers in the capital. His part in the proceedings at this time was vital.

The Bolshevik take-over On 10 October Lenin returned in secret from Finland and convinced the party that the time had come to seize power. On 21 October the Petrograd garrison recognized the Soviet as the sole lawful power. On the 23rd the Peter and Paul fortress with 100 000 rifles went over to the Soviet. The coming revolution was widely known and Kerensky tried unsuccessfully to arrest the Military Revolutionary Committee and the Bolshevik leaders.

Red Guards storming the Winter Palace

The last orders went out from Bolshevik headquarters in the Smolny Institute on 24 October. During that night bands of armed Red Guards seized the most important points in the city — the power stations, the telegraph offices, the railway stations, the State bank, the bridges over the river Neva. As the citizens woke up on the 25th they found the power of the Provisional Government fast disappearing. Kerensky had left the capital to try to rally support outside. By midday the only major building not seized was the Provisional Government's headquarters in the Winter Palace. A few blank salvoes from the Cruiser *Aurora*, brought up the River Neva by Bolshevik supporters, showed that resistance was useless, and the women's guard defending the palace surrendered. A group of Red Guards rushed into the palace and demanded submission from the Provisional Government. This was finally obtained at 2.10 on the morning of 26 October. The Provisional Government declared that 'members submit to force and surrender in order to avoid bloodshed'. They were promptly arrested. The Bolsheviks were now in power.

Why the   The Provisional Government had lasted only eight months. Born in hope,
Provisional   it had failed to provide the two things the Russian people wanted above all —
Government fell peace and land.

The disastrous war with Germany had been caused by inefficiencies, mainly a lack of industrial production and a breakdown in the transport system. There was little the Provisional Government could do to remedy that situation in a few months. Should they, therefore, have made peace? When they called for peace the majority of Russians were expressing a cry from the heart. But when it came to practicalities few wanted 'peace at any price'. Even the Bolsheviks presumed peace would be made on fair terms with representatives of the German workers and soldiers, not with the Kaiser. It is highly unlikely that the government would have long survived the kind of peace that the Bolsheviks later accepted at Brest-Litovsk. So instead of peace the Provisional government launched a final summer offensive, saw it fail, and then witnessed the disintegration of the armed forces, a process promoted by Order No. 1 of the Petrograd Soviet as well as by the military disasters.

After peace, the Provisional Government was preparing for the meeting of the Constituent Assembly and for reform — the elections were in fact planned for mid-November. Very little reform had been achieved by the time the government fell. The food shortages remained acute. The Provisional Government has been criticized for not carrying out a distribution of the land among the peasants, but would it have been sensible to do so while they were still trying to win the war? The Russian army was basically a peasant army, and such a step would undoubtedly have led to its break-up. When the peasants did begin to seize the nobles' lands, either on their own initiative or through the Soviets, the government lacked the will and probably the ability to prevent them, and during the summer of 1917 disorder in the countryside spread fast.

The government was loath to use repressive methods akin to Tsarist practices to keep order. When Kerensky finally realized that the situation required firm action and possibly suspension of some of the liberties given in the early days of the revolution, it was too late. The more conservative elements in the government and the army leaders thought him too weak and too socialist; they relied instead on General Kornilov to bring the situation under control. To save himself against Kornilov, Kerensky thus found himself relying on forces that eventually wanted to bring him down. The Bolsheviks were freed and armed. Kerensky was losing control of Russia and in the rising anarchy it took only a determined armed group to take advantage of the situation. The revolutionary Bolsheviks, with their increasing support among the soldiers and workers of the major cities, were just such a group. Convinced by Lenin of the necessity of seizing power, and organized by Trotsky, they acted quickly in the days 24 October to 26 October.* Kerensky, just like the Tsar before him, found few ready to fight to save his government. After a brief attempt to march on Petrograd with some Cossack soldiers had petered out, he fled to the USA where he lived on until 1970.

The strains of a minor war had shaken the autocratic Tsarist regime in 1905; those of a major war had brought it down 12 years later; the problems of war had now destroyed its democratically-minded successor.

---

* The dates used in this chapter are in the old style. The Russian calendar (the Julian) was 13 days behind the Western (the Gregorian) calendar, until the Bolsheviks brought them into line in February 1918 (1 February becoming 14 February). It would be correct therefore to talk of the March and November revolutions as opposed to the February and October ones.

3
The Establishment and Survival of the Communist State: Russia, 1917–24

(1) Bolshevik Dictatorship

The Bolshevik take-over in Petrograd had cost few lives. The seizure of power in Moscow which followed was far more bloody; there was a week's fierce fighting before Moscow too fell to the Bolsheviks.

The new government faced two major tasks. The first was an immediate practical problem: to maintain themselves in power and extend their rule beyond the towns already seized, and to get the Russian people to obey them. How were 300 000 Bolsheviks to control a country of 130 million people? The second concern went deeper. How quickly and in which way were they to carry out the transformation of Russian society along Marxist lines? Marx had assumed that the country in which a successful revolution occurred would be predominantly industrial and that the first years would see a dictatorship of the industrial proletariat (see p. 6); but Russia was still predominantly agricultural.

The Bolsheviks had to see what was feasible. In opposition they had been quite clear on what they wished to do with Russia. Once in power they had to concern themselves not just with broad strategy, but also with the day-to-day business of governing. Perhaps some of their aims would have to be delayed or even dropped as impracticable. Certainly the new government was very determined; it assumed it had all the answers, and had only scorn for doubters. They had no real intention of sharing power with any other party. The All-Russian Congress of Soviets, which met on the days of the Petrograd take-over, contained many Mensheviks and Socialist Revolutionaries who disagreed with the use of force to gain power. They were fiercely attacked by Trotsky.

> You are pitiful isolated individuals. You are bankrupts, your role is played out. Go where you belong from now on . . . onto the rubbish heap of History.

The dictatorship of the proletariat soon became the dictatorship of the Bolshevik Party, which was renamed the Communist Party in early 1918. Officially, law-making powers remained with the All-Russian Congress of Soviets, but all the decisions that mattered were made by the small cabinet of ministers, or Commissars as they became known, headed by Lenin. Other figures of importance in 1917 included Leon Trotsky as Commissar for Foreign Affairs, and Joseph Stalin as Commissar for the Nationalities, responsible for the welfare of the different peoples within the Russian state.

Decrees on peace and land   In the first days of power, decrees were proclaimed on the two supreme issues of the time. The first called for a truce with Germany and for the making of a just peace 'without annexations or indemnities', a peace to be obtained, hopefully, after a communist revolution of the German workers had succeeded. The second declared that the land was nationalized and was to be taken over by the poorer peasants as arranged by the village Soviets. This was not the Marxist ideal, which wanted co-operative farms, where there would be no private ownership and where the units of production would be large enough to produce vast quantities of food for the workers in the towns. The land decree was a temporary practicality which ensured some kind of mass support for the new government and got rid of the power of the landlords, who by their very nature would be against the revolution.

Businesses nationalized   In the following months further decrees altered the structure of the economy and society. The most important sectors of the economy were nationalized; the banks, transport, foreign trade, fuel and power. The factories were to be run by elected committees of the workers; the old owners and managers were removed. An eight-hour day became law. All titles were abolished and 'comrade' become the normal form of address. The old Tsarist legal system was abolished and a new court system was established to bring greater justice to the people. Women were declared equal at law with men. The strict marriage and divorce laws were relaxed; divorce could be had for the asking. Illegitimate children were to have the same rights as those born of married parents. The different nationalities within the old Tsarist empire were given the right to rule themselves and to decide their own future. The Russian Orthodox Church, which had been one of the Tsar's

'Equality'

The Church and religion   pillars of support, was stripped of all its power. Its lands were nationalized, and its right to control education was withdrawn. Religious education in state schools vanished. Marriages in church were no longer valid; only civil marriage was now legal. The Church underwent a period of severe persecution in the first years of the revolution. Local Soviets often smashed up churches, seized their riches and attacked the priests. Religious worship was actively discouraged and the press was used to discredit religion and the clergy.

Censorship   Whereas Kerensky had not been willing to bring in restrictions on liberty to help him retain power, the new government showed no such hesitation. Press censorship was soon revived, the Bolsheviks being only too well aware how their own propaganda had helped bring down the Provisional Government. In December 1917 a new secret police force under the Pole, Felix Dzerzshinsky, was established. It was known as Cheka, an abbreviation from the Russian for the All-Russian Extraordinary Commission for Fighting Counter-Revolutionary Sabotage, and it was to seek out and deal with enemies of the government.

'Cheka'

The Constituent Assembly   The elections for a Russian Parliament, which the Provisional Government had fixed for November, were allowed to take place. Lenin had been against holding them as he knew the Bolsheviks could not hope to win a majority, but he was overruled. The Bolsheviks gained about a quarter of the votes cast (mainly in the industrial centres and the armed forces) and with their Left-Socialist Revolutionary allies they had 215 seats out of 707. The largest party was the party of the peasants, the moderate Socialist Revolutionaries. The assembly met in January 1918 and failed to ratify the laws so far decreed by the government. The non-Bolshevik speakers found themselves howled down by Bolshevik supporters and soldiers and sailors in the galleries. After one day the assembly was dispersed by force. It never met again. The Communist government was not going to allow the Russians the luxury of a Western-style democracy. This dismissal of the Constituent Assembly brought the prospect of a full-scale civil war much nearer.

Revolutionary poster hailing the dawn of the new age

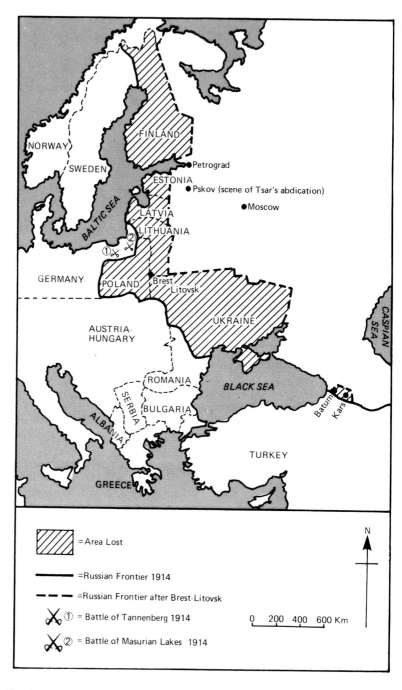

NORWAY

SWEDEN

FINLAND

●Petrograd

ESTONIA

●Pskov (scene of Tsar's abdication)

●Moscow

LATVIA

LITHUANIA

BALTIC SEA

GERMANY

POLAND

Brest Litovsk

AUSTRIA-HUNGARY

UKRAINE

CASPIAN SEA

ROMANIA

SERBIA

BULGARIA

BLACK SEA

ALBANIA

Batum

Kars

TURKEY

GREECE

////// = Area Lost

———— = Russian Frontier 1914

— — — = Russian Frontier after Brest-Litovsk

✕ ① = Battle of Tannenberg 1914

✕ ② = Battle of Masurian Lakes 1914

N

0 200 400 600 Km

The Treaty of Brest-Litovsk, 1918; this disastrous peace treaty deprived Russia of much of her industry and best agricultural land — it is little wonder that Lenin planned to ignore it at the first possible opportunity

(2) The Treaty of Brest-Litovsk (1918)

The question of how and when to end the war was of paramount importance. Lenin was for making peace as soon as possible on the best terms that could be obtained. An armistice with the German Command was agreed in December 1917 and Trotsky began the serious negotiations at Brest-Litovsk in Poland in January 1918. The Germans, triumphant in the east, were keen to make peace in order to be able to transfer their armies to the west. But they drove a cruel bargain. They demanded Poland and the Baltic provinces, and they also backed a claim by the Ukrainians for their independence. The Ukraine was important, as it produced vast quantities of grain as well as most of Russia's coal and metal output. Lenin thought the Russians should accept, fearing lest a further German advance would not only take more territory but also unseat the Communist government. Trotsky had the majority of the government with him in his ploy of playing for time, and when the Germans finally lost patience and demanded acceptance of their terms, Trotsky astounded them by announcing that Russia would make 'neither peace — nor war'. The Germans easily demonstrated the weakness of Trotsky's policy by launching a new offensive in mid-February*. The Russian capital was moved from Petrograd to Moscow as a precaution. It has remained there ever since, the seat of government being the old fortress and palace of the Kremlin. Lenin was now able to carry the government with him for accepting the German peace terms, even though it was still a very close vote. Trotsky resigned as Commissar for Foreign Affairs, and Sokolnikov signed for Russia at Brest-Litovsk on 3 March 1918.

The final peace terms were extremely harsh. Russia lost Finland, Poland, the Ukraine, and the Baltic provinces of Latvia, Lithuania and Estonia. An area in the Caucasus around Kars and Batum went to Turkey. At the stroke of a pen Russia was deprived of a third of her population, a third of her best farming land, a third of her factories and three-quarters of her coal- and iron-producing areas. She also had to pay reparations totalling 3000 million roubles in gold. Lenin had no intention of keeping to the treaty. He said he would ignore it at the first possible opportunity, but he believed that signing it was necessary in order to give the Communist government a breathing space so that it could keep its hold on Russia.

(3) The Civil War and Foreign Intervention, 1918–21

The 'Whites'   In 1918 a variety of different groups opposed Communist rule in Russia. There were those including the moderate Socialist Revolutionaries and Mensheviks who resented the Communist dictatorship, as expressed in the dismissal of the Constituent Assembly in January with its evident disregard for the wishes of the Russian people. Others were against the wholesale confiscation of property and businesses which the government had implemented. A few wished to see the Tsar restored. To these opponents of the regime were now added those who could no longer support a government which had made such a disastrous peace for Russia at Brest-Litovsk.

---

*At this stage in 1918 the dates of the Russian and Western calendars coincide. The Russian 1 February became 14 February.

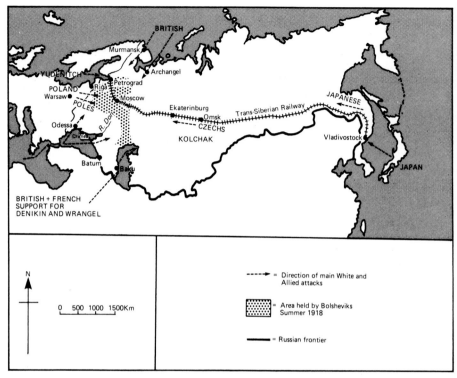

The Civil War and foreign intervention (1918–21); initially the Reds held only a very small area of Russia around the major cities

By the beginning of 1918 the Communists were supreme in most of European Russia, including the major cities such as Moscow and Petrograd. Elsewhere were huge areas where they had yet to secure full control. In these areas various groups or individuals now began to declare themselves unwilling to recognize the government in Moscow. Instead they set up their own governments, and began to organize themselves into fighting forces to secure their survival and to bring down the Communists. They became known collectively as the Whites (opposed to the Reds, the Communists) and, by the summer of 1918, a full-scale and bloody civil war had erupted. Many of the leaders of the Whites were ex-Tsarist officers, such as Admiral Kolchak, who established a military dictatorship in central Russia at Omsk, and General Denikin, who set himself up in the Don region of southern Russia. At one stage there were as many as 18 different groups calling themselves 'the government of Russia'.

Foreign intervention   The situation was complicated for the Reds by the intervention of foreign powers in support of the Whites. Russia's allies in the First World War — Britain, France, and the United States — were greatly disappointed at Russia's exit from the war. Although the Russians had won few victories, their efforts on the eastern front had kept huge numbers of German troops pinned down. These could now be transferred to the west. The Western Allies, therefore, would have welcomed a different government in Russia, one which would re-open the war against Germany. Moreover, they had no wish whatever to see a regime established which preached world-wide revolution and the destruction of capitalist systems like their own. The French had a further quarrel with the Bolsheviks, as the Communist government had refused to pay all foreign debts incurred by the Tsarist regime and had taken over foreign capital invested in Russia. Most of this money had been French.

BOLSHEVIKS DEFEATED NEAR ARCHANGEL.

GALLANT FIGHTING BY OUR MEN AGAINST A "DECISIVE" ATTACK.

NEW HOPES OF RELIEF.

Heavy attacks have been made by the Bolsheviks on our troops in the Archangel region, but have been defeated with great gallantry. No movement is reported near Murmansk.

Hopes of relieving the Allied forces in North Russia have increased. There are signs of thaw at Archangel, which would put a stop to the Bolshevist attacks by land. The thaw will afford an opportunity for attacks by armed Bolshevist steamers travelling down the River Dvina. That part of the river held by the Bolsheviks becomes free of ice before the part held by the Allies, but Allied naval detachments are ready to co-operate when they can. A most important factor is the wind. If it blows from the west or south-west there will be a clear channel through the White Sea early in May.

The hardships which have been suffered by B and C category men in the Arctic winter are described by a soldier who has returned to London.

FIVE ATTACKS BY BOLSHEVIKS.

READY FOR RIVER FIGHTING.

LIFE IN BELL TENTS IN ARCTIC WINTER.

SUFFERINGS OF B AND C MEN ON THE MURMAN COAST.

66 DEGREES OF FROST

The hardships which are being endured by the many low-category men in the British force on the Murman coast were described to a "Daily Express" representative yesterday by a London Territorial who has returned from Murmansk. He said :—

I went out in the City of Marseilles last June. There were 600 men on board, and all were low-category men—B 2, and some C. I belonged to a set of 220 men and three officers who had been stationed at Clacton-on-Sea for a long time —" wash-outs " of the 29th City of London Regiment (Royal Fusiliers). We had been employed as officers' servants or in the sergeants' mess, the tailors' shops or cook-houses, and had done no soldiering for a considerable time, but we were sent to Colchester, rushed through three weeks' training, and then packed off to the Murman coast.

MOSQUITOES.

In July and August we had almost tropical heat and mosquitoes, while in

The Daily Express on the Civil War, 1919

Trotsky and the Red Army   To face and defeat such an array of opponents so soon after coming to power posed a huge problem for the Bolsheviks. The Tsarist army had all but disintegrated and a new Red Army was brought into being in January 1918. It consisted initially of volunteers, but soon compulsory military service was introduced for workers and peasants aged 18–40. Conscription had only been abolished in 1917 and its re-introduction was most unpopular. Few Russians had much enthusiasm for a further war and discipline was difficult to enforce. That the Red Army did not actually fall apart was due mainly to one man, Leon Trotsky, appointed Commissar for War in March 1918. His tireless efforts and enthusiasm quickly moulded a respectable fighting force. Where exhortation and praise failed, he was quite prepared to use terror. Desertion again became punishable by death and, when the troops went into action, Cheka units went behind them ready to deal with any of the less enthusiastic! By 1920 the Reds had five million troops in the field.

The Bolshevik view of foreign intervention in the Civil War — British, French and American characters hold the leashes of dogs labelled Denikin, Kolchak and Yudenich

The initial Allied intervention was justified as necessary to stop arms supplies, sent by them for Russia's war effort, from falling into German hands. But the forces which landed in the north at Archangel and Murmansk soon gave full support to the Whites in those areas. Later in 1918, there was Allied intervention in the south as well — the British in the oil-rich areas of Batum and Baku, the French at Odessa. The Japanese joined in, landing in the far east at Vladivostock, seeing an opportunity to increase their empire in that area — a step as much opposed by the Americans, who had also intervened, as by the Russians. The Czechs too, became involved in a major way. They had been subjects of the Austro-Hungarian Empire in 1914 and many had given themselves up to the Russians to form a Czech legion in the hope of fighting against the Austrians to win their independence. When the civil war broke out they were on their way by train to Vladivostock, with the intention of making a sea passage to France, to join the British and French forces fighting the Germans and Austrians. Relations between them and the Communist government soon became strained. When Trotsky demanded that they give up their weapons they refused to do so. Instead they took over parts of the Trans-Siberian railway and joined the Whites.

Trotsky was a great believer in using experts and it was his idea to recruit ex-Tsarist officers into the Red Army. They were strange leaders for such an openly class-based force, but to ensure that they did not act treacherously, political commissars were appointed alongside them to keep watch on them and to confirm, or reject, their orders. Forty-eight thousand Tsarist officers were recruited, about four-fifths of the total number of commanders.

During the war Trotsky rushed from one front to another, supervising the war effort. He went in a special train which contained a printing press for publishing information and propaganda, radio and telegraph apparatus, cars for travelling to areas away from the line, and a machine-gun unit. This centre of operations required two engines to pull it along.

1919 — the turning point

The year 1919 proved to be difficult for the Reds as White forces threatened on all sides. Kolchak attacked from the east, Denikin from the south, and Yudenich from the west. Denikin's forces got to within 320 kilometres of Moscow before being driven back, and only Trotsky's personal involvement in the defence of Petrograd saved the city from Yudenich's forces. However, by the end of 1919, the Whites had been driven back and the war had definitely turned in the Reds' favour. The following year saw a gradual advance turn into total victory for the Communists despite Polish intervention.

Polish intervention

The Poles used the opportunity of Russian weakness to try to extend their lands beyond those allotted to them at the Peace of Versailles. Led by Pilsudski, they crossed into Russia in April 1920, but after initial successes they were driven out again. Lenin, against the advice of Trotsky and Stalin, saw an opportunity to spread the revolution. Russian forces pushed towards the Polish capital, Warsaw, but they were in turn driven back. The hoped-for workers' rising did not materialize. Russia, therefore, made peace with Poland by the treaty of Riga 1921, losing land in the west to the new Polish state. By this stage the Civil War in Russia was virtually over (although the last Japanese troops did not leave Russian territory until October 1922).

Why the Reds won

The Red Army had succeeded against what had appeared to be overwhelming odds. The reasons for this need closer study. Strategically the Communists were in the stronger position. The Whites tended to be fighting from the outlying areas, moving towards the centre, and their lines of communication were inclined to be long. Co-ordination between their different forces was minimal. The Reds, controlling the central area, had the benefit of shorter lines and could also make better use of the railways, which were based on Moscow and Petrograd.

White disunity

The opposition to the Reds was known collectively as the Whites, but the various groups who made up the Whites had little in common, except their wish to bring down the Communists. How they would rule Russia when this was achieved was hotly disputed. Some of the White leaders, such as Denikin and Kolchak, set up harsh military dictatorships in their areas and brought back the rule of the landlords. They also treated the non-Russian people of the state as inferior to the Russians. These actions lost the Whites much support from the peasants and the non-Russians; they also led to rebellions against White rule by their former allies, the Socialist Revolutionaries. On top of these policy differences there were also personal rivalries. The Czechs, for example, quarrelled with Admiral Kolchak and handed him over to the Bolsheviks, who promptly shot him. In the south Denikin was forced to give way to General Wrangel.

Red unity

The Reds in contrast were unified in purpose and policy. Their land policy ultimately gave them considerable peasant support, for only a Red victory would guarantee the peasants possession of their recently won land. The Bolsheviks also made great play of the rights of the different peoples to decide their own future and to preserve their language and customs. The Communist leadership proved more skilful, and Trotsky above all must take particular credit for the Red victory. He was responsible for the military successes while Lenin and others provided the required economic and political support.

Withdrawal of foreign troops   The intervention of the foreign powers was in the long run not able to alter the outcome of the Civil War. When the First World War came to an end with the defeat of Germany in November 1918, one of the major reasons for intervention — to get Russia back into the war — was gone. The Allies did not have the will to fight on in Russia after the massive sacrifices they had already made. Some major political figures, such as Foch in France and Churchill in Britain, wished to wipe out Bolshevism before it had a chance to spread. Churchill said, 'If we don't put our foot on the egg, we shall have to chase the chicken round the farmyard of the world'. But this was not a popular view and British and French troops were gradually withdrawn from Soviet territory during 1919. After an incident in the Crimea when their sailors hoisted the Red Flag, the French were also concerned that what they saw as the Bolshevik germ might infect their own forces. The foreign powers continued, however, to supply vast quantities of war materials to the Whites, and, by so doing, were able to prolong their war efforts. Yet the Reds were able to make some political gains from the foreign involvement, claiming they were the only truly Russian party, while the Whites were the slaves of foreign imperialists.

(4) War Communism and Political Control

The restructuring of Russian society had been started by the splitting up of the estates of the landlords in 1917. The Communists intended originally to transform society gradually at a realistic pace. But the continuing food shortages, which had affected the towns for the whole of 1917, and the demands of the civil war effort, meant that the plans had to be drastically altered and greater state direction imposed.

The food problem   Food was the most pressing problem. Not enough food was getting through to the towns. This was partly due to transport difficulties; but the main reason was that the peasants did not wish to sell their surpluses for money, since the rouble was quickly losing value, and there was little being produced to spend their money on anyway. Consequently there was not enough food to sustain the Red Army soldiers and factory workers. The town dwellers drifted away into the countryside to find food; and industrial production, so vital for the war effort, declined. The government therefore

Grain requisitioning   decided that the excess food being produced would have to be seized and Food Armies, often with *Cheka* support, were given orders accordingly. Committees of the poor were established in the villages to spy on people who might be hoarding grain to sell on the black market at a high profit. Many unco-operative peasants were shot while others destroyed their crops rather than hand them over for nothing, and sowed less the following year. Food production dropped, and it remained a desperate problem for the Communists throughout the Civil War, especially as many of the best grain-growing areas were held by the Whites.

Further nationalization   The necessities of war also speeded up the take-over of industry. In June 1918 all large-scale industry was nationalized without compensation, and by the end of the year this was extended to all enterprises employing 10 or more workers. Local Soviets often extended this further to include all enterprises in their area. All private trade was officially abolished, although in the chaos of civil war a black market remained and, in fact, kept many people alive.

Ration cards The government steadily tightened its control of industry. Control over the labour force was exercised by the use of ration cards. Those not producing their own food were allotted rations according to their usefulness. Soldiers and workers got the largest slice, professional people less, and 'class enemies', such as ex-nobles, got none at all. These people were reduced to bartering their possessions on the black market. As the war progressed the workforce was treated like a mobilized army, directed to where it was needed. Strikes were declared to be illegal. These controls over agriculture and industry, associated with the period of the Civil War (1918–21), became known as War Communism.

Increased As control of the economy increased so too did the hold of the government political control on political life. In the early part of 1918 Lenin still allowed criticism of his policies, notably the peace treaty, by his Left Socialist Revolutionary allies. But the Civil War put an end to the last remains of the limited political freedoms, as more and more groups joined the Whites. In July 1918 the Left Socialist Revolutionaries, increasingly hostile to the Bolsheviks, planned risings in Moscow. They were put down. Then on 30 August the head of the Petrograd *Cheka* was assassinated, and on the same day in Moscow, Lenin was shot at and injured by a woman called Fanya Kaplan. These events, against the background of a developing Civil War, led to a policy of whole-sale terror. *Cheka* was given full powers to search out and deal with enemies of the revolution. Socialist Revolutionaries and persons suspected of plotting against the government were not the only ones to be shot. Thousands of 'class enemies' suffered a similar fate. Former landlords, factory owners, priests and the like were shot, not for what they had done, but simply for being what they were.

Murder of the It was in the summer of 1918 too that Nicholas, the ex-Tsar, and his family Tsar were murdered by their Communist guards at Ekaterinburg in the Urals. The orders did not come from Moscow; they were decisions taken locally as Czech troops advanced on the town. The whole royal family and their personal servants were ushered into a cellar and gunned down. Their bodies were destroyed by acid and fire and their remains scattered down a mine shaft. There were to be no graves at which their supporters could come and pay their respects — no martyrs' tombs.*

(5) The New Economic Policy of 1921

The Civil War was virtually over by 1921. The Reds had won. They now presided over a country torn by three years of national war, two revolutions, and three years of Civil War. Russia was in ruins: industry was at a stand-still; agricultural production was down by almost a half; the currency was worthless; and most of the railway rolling stock was out of action. An

*This account of the Tsar's death has been disputed in *File on the Tsar* by A. Summers and T. Mangold (Fontana, 1977). They have suggested that at least the Tsarina and her daughters escaped.

estimated 28 million had died in the fighting, or from epidemics and starvation. The priority was now to rebuild Russia and to give her a period of stability and recovery. A huge plan for electrification was introduced in 1920 with the aim of building 30 large power stations in the following 15 years. But the great question now was whether the state would, or even could, keep tight control of the economy as a means of organizing its recovery. The Russian peasantry had certainly had enough of grain requisitioning by the government. In the countryside there was increasing violence against those sent to seize the food, and it reached the point when serious rebellions began to break out.

The 'Kronstadt rising'

There was trouble in the cities too, not least in Petrograd, where in February 1921 the workers came out on strike against the policies of War Communism. Then in March, the sailors at Kronstadt, 'the pride and glory of the revolution', as Lenin had called them, rose against the government demanding an end to the Communist Party dictatorship, and Communist domination of the Soviets. They wanted freedom of election, of speech, of assembly for all the left-wing parties. The Kronstadt sailors had always been at the forefront of Bolshevik support and their discontent was of great significance. Lenin presented the revolt of the sailors as a White plot, and Trotsky ordered the army across the ice to smash the resistance, but this rising was, as Lenin said, 'the flash which lit up reality better than anything else'.

NEP

Lenin had been considering a relaxation in the economy and the Kronstadt uprising led to the introduction of the New Economic Policy of 1921. Everything, including Marxist ideals, had to be set aside to increase production. People were no longer to be asked to work solely for the common good; in future they were also to be allowed to work for their own personal gain.

The main features of the policy were as follows. Firstly, the peasants were to remain in possession of the land. Grain requisitioning was to cease, but a certain amount of the peasants' produce was to be paid to the government as a tax; they were free to sell any surplus on the open market for their own profit. Private trade was allowed again. The incentive of a private profit, it was hoped, would encourage people to grow more and push up agricultural production. In 1922 farmers were even allowed to hire labour again, a practice previously forbidden as producing a class system.

Secondly, all industrial and business enterprises employing less than 20 people were denationalized. They were to be returned to their former owners or leased to individuals or co-operatives, so that here again private initiative and the profit motive could encourage economic recovery.

Thirdly, the heavy industries such as coal, iron and steel production, power, transport, foreign trade, the banks — 'the commanding heights' of the economy — were to remain nationalized under government control. Yet even here there was to be a change. Workers' control had not proved very successful since the workers did not have sufficient skill to run their factories, and now former managers were put in charge again as 'specialists', and they were encouraged to do well by special payments. 'Class enemies' had their uses.

In agriculture the results of the NEP were delayed a year because of a terrible drought in the Volga region in 1921. Probably a further five million Russians died of starvation, despite enormous amounts of foreign aid from the Red Cross and Herbert Hoover's American Relief Administration. After this disaster, agricultural production picked up and many peasants did very well for themselves; they were known as 'kulaks'.

Under NEP Russia had her much-needed period of stability and recovery. Industrial and agricultural output reached pre-First World War levels by about 1926. Private traders and businessmen became known as 'Nepmen' and many became rich. Many foreigners assumed that Russia was gradually returning to capitalism. Lenin even tried to encourage foreign investment again (with little success), in complete contradiction to everything Marxism was supposed to stand for.

(6) The USSR and its Government

The 1924 Constitution

After the introduction of the 1918 Constitution Russia was in theory a democracy, with all workers and peasants allowed to vote for their local Soviets which in turn sent delegates to the All-Russian Congress of Soviets. A new constitution along similar lines, which was largely Stalin's work, came into operation in 1924 for all the lands now under Russian control. This set up four Soviet Socialist republics (Russia, Transcaucasia, the Ukraine and Byelorussia) in a Union of Soviet Socialist Republics — the USSR. The separate republics had some power over local affairs, but the central government kept control of most important matters, such as military and foreign affairs, foreign trade, the national economy, transport and communications. Since 1917 the Communists had always stressed the right of the different peoples in the state to decide their own future. This was now repeated in the Constitution, though in practice it was never allowed.

A French view of life in Soviet Russia (1935)

The administrative structure was rather like a pyramid with four layers, with village Soviets at the bottom. Then came the city or county Soviets; above them the Soviets of territories, provinces and republics; and at the top the All Union Congress of Soviets. The system was in theory democratic. The village Soviets were elected by all over 18 years old, excluding such people as priests, and the higher levels of government were chosen from the layers below. The All Union Congress had supreme power, but with over 2000 members it was too unwieldy to function effectively, so it in turn chose an All Union Central Executive Committee which met three times a year, and this then elected a Presidium of 27 members to carry on day-to-day government. From this body came the Cabinet of Ministers, or *Sovnarkom*.

The role of the party   Each level of government was filled by members of the Communist Party, and it was in the party therefore, that real power lay. As with the government there were many levels of organisation from local committees through to the party Congress. The latter chose one-tenth of its number as a Central Committee and this in turn chose the leadership, which was organised into a Political Section, or Politburo, headed by the Chairman of the party, and the Organizational Bureau headed by the General Secretary. The General Secretary was very influential because he usually advised the government on whom to appoint to important jobs — from those in the Civil Service to newspaper editors. Stalin filled this post from 1922.

In theory the different layers of organization in the government and party, from the small local groups to the central body, allowed local ideas to make their way up through the structure; government would then be representative of the people. In practice, the layers of organization were used for passing ideas and orders down and the country was dictated to by the Communist Party leadership.

While the economy was relaxed in 1921 the political system was tightened up. The Kronstadt sailors had demanded freedom for all left-wing parties, but this was rejected, and the Socialist Revolutionary and Menshevik Parties, which had managed to survive, were now outlawed. The only legal party was the Communist Party. This had always been limited to those who were considered 'politically sound', and there were periodic reviews when the party was 'cleansed' or purged of undesirable or unreliable members. In 1921 a fifth of the party, 136 000 members, were expelled. At the same time the leadership cut down on the freedom of party members to criticize the official party line. Organized opposition groups within the party were forbidden. It also became possible for the Central Committee to throw out people who had been elected by the party Congress, a power they could now use to expel anyone whose ideas they did not like. The apparatus whereby the top party officials dictated to the rest of the party therefore became established. Stalin was later to use this procedure to full and deadly effect against many of the people who were now voting for this change.

The bureaucracy   In a country where the central government was taking increasing control there were large numbers of officials or bureaucrats. The structure of the civil service became increasingly complex, and the amount of red tape and the slowness of decision making proved a major problem. An inspectorate (*Rabkrin*) headed by Joseph Stalin had been established in 1919 to watch over the work of government departments, to make sure they worked efficiently and fairly. This inspectorate became as bureaucratic as the civil service it was set up to watch over. It was very like Tsarist days: people sent pleas to Lenin, as they had done to the Tsar, asking him to take up their particular cases with one or other of the government departments in order to secure a fair decision for them. Lenin was very worried about this trend in his later years. He was concerned that government was becoming increasingly divorced from the people it was supposed to serve.

(7) The Bolsheviks and Europe after 1917

In the first years after the October Revolution Soviet foreign policy was concerned with extricating Russia from the First World War and making peace with Germany at Brest-Litovsk. Immediately after this, at a time when the new regime was struggling to survive in the Civil War, foreign policy was dominated by the involvement of a host of foreign powers supporting the Russian Whites. More widely, the Russian Communists predicted and hoped for workers' revolutions in the industrially advanced nations of western Europe, especially in Germany where the disruptions of the war had brought unrest. They assumed initially that the survival of a communist regime in peasant Russia would depend on similar revolutions occurring elsewhere, for a communist regime could not survive in a totally hostile world. To hasten the world-wide revolution the Communist International, or *Comintern*, with representatives of many different countries, was estab-

Comintern established

lished in Moscow in 1919. A set of delegates, who were not particularly representative of the communist world, elected Zinoviev as its first president.

Various attempted Communist take-overs took place and in 1919 'Red' republics were actually established in Germany, in Berlin and Bavaria, and in Hungary. These, however, proved very short-lived, and as Europe settled down after the war, the likelihood of Communist success outside Russia was minimal. There was little hope of further revolution and in the process of trying to encourage it the Russian regime incurred the suspicion of other powers and caused a united hostile bloc to form against her. This was clearly not in Russia's interest and by 1920 there were signs of a changing policy. Treaties of friendship were signed by Russia with several of her neighbours, including Estonia, Finland, Persia (now Iran), Afghanistan and Turkey. In the last three cases, mention was made of a joint effort to fight Western imperialism and exploitation. Russia was presenting herself as the champion of the exploited and underprivileged nations of the world, even though most of them were very anti-Communist.

By the Third Congress of *Comintern* (1921) the policy of world-wide revolution had been watered down. Russia and her Commissar for Foreign Affairs, Chicherin, began working for recognition of the Bolshevik regime and for treaties which would bring Russia economic aid. Russia was now entering upon the New Economic Policy and wanted Western technology through trade and, if possible, loans of money. Further treaties were signed with more neighbours and also with Great Britain in 1921, yet these negotiations were hampered by the Western demand that the Communists pay back Tsarist debts and give compensation for the foreign property they had nationalized since 1917.

Treaty of Rapallo with Germany

Soviet Russia had not been invited to join the League of Nations, nor would she at that stage have wanted to join a capitalist international organization. She was not invited to the international disarmament conference at Washington in 1921; she was, however, represented at the Genoa economic conference of European powers in 1922. The negotiations here failed, but at the same time an agreement was worked out with the German government at Rapallo (April 1922). The two outcast and distrusted nations of Europe agreed to renounce all claims against each other, to establish diplomatic relations, and to promote economic co-operation. Secretly, they also agreed to arrangements whereby the Germans evaded the military clauses of the Versailles treaty by manufacturing ammunition and training soldiers on Russian soil.

Meanwhile, the policy of encouraging revolution was not entirely dropped, although two Comintern-inspired risings in Germany and Estonia in 1923 were dismal failures, and merely encouraged the growth of fervently anti-communist parties.

(8) The Last Years of Lenin, and an Assessment

Lenin's illness

In May 1922 Lenin suffered a major stroke. This was followed in December by a second which left him paralysed down his right side. As he slowly recovered he was aware that he had not long to live and he became very concerned with the future. In particular he was worried about the party leadership after his death. He felt that none of the Politburo members would make an entirely suitable successor. He considered Trotsky and Stalin as the two most able men, but he had fault to find with each. In his dictated 'Testament' he said of Stalin:

His 'Political Testament'

> Comrade Stalin, having become General Secretary, has concentrated enormous power in his hands, and I am not sure that he always knows how to use that power with sufficient caution.

Of Trotsky, he said,

> distinguished not only by his exceptional abilities — personally he is, to be sure, the most able man in the present Central Committee — but also by his too far-reaching self-confidence, and a disposition to be too much attracted by the purely administrative side of affairs.

He was worried that the party might become split around these two with neither able to hold together the divergent personalities and views of the Central Committee in the same way as he himself could.

Attempt to remove Stalin

As 1923 opened Lenin became increasingly alarmed at Stalin's growing power and the way in which he was using it. The latter had kept Lenin isolated from political news during his recent illness. He had also been extremely rude to Krupskaya, Lenin's wife. Evidence was coming to light that suggested high-handed action and bullying against the people of his native Georgia, whose independence under Menshevik rule had just been crushed by the Red Army on Stalin's orders. In early January Lenin dictated further views on Stalin:

> Stalin is too rude, and this fault, entirely supportable in relations among us

Communists, becomes insupportable in the office of General Secretary. Therefore, I propose to the comrades to find a way to remove Stalin from that position and to appoint to it another man, who in all respects, differs from Stalin only in superiority, namely, more patient, more loyal, more polite, and more attentive to comrades, less capricious etc.

By March he was preparing, with Trotsky, an attack on Stalin at the 12th Party Congress. The attack never took place for Lenin suffered yet another stroke and this one left him severly paralysed and unable to speak. His political life was over. In October 1923 he was well enough to be driven to his office in the Kremlin for a short visit, but within an hour of yet another stroke on 21 January 1924, he was dead.

Lenin dies Lenin died a national hero. Many thousands of ordinary Russians came to Moscow to pay their respects and to file past his embalmed body. He was laid to rest in a giant mausoleum in Red Square in central Moscow, and his tomb has become a place of pilgrimage for Communists. The city of Petrograd was renamed Leningrad in his honour.

Lenin's funeral

An assessment There is no doubt that in his lifetime Lenin stood head and shoulders above other members of his party. One could imagine the party without any of them, whereas the Communist Party without Lenin would have seemed an impossibility. It was he who had developed the theories of organized revolution, which had split the Russian Social Democratic Party back in 1903, and he who had held the Bolsheviks together during the hopeless years of 1906–17. He had returned to Russia in April 1917 and had, with his 'April

Theses', set the party on a policy of non-co-operation with the Provisional government. He was determined to use the opportunities offered in late 1917 to push for a second revolution, and when the Bolsheviks had a majority in the Petrograd and Moscow Soviets and when Kerensky's support was slipping away, he returned from Finland to convince the Central Committee of the need to seize power.

Following the October Revolution he was at the centre of decision-making, arguing with and persuading his comrades that his views on how to set about developing communism in Russia were the correct ones. He master-minded the establishment of the Communist dictatorship, and won basic peasant support by his decrees on land, peace and the nationalities. He insisted on the peace being signed with Germany in March 1918. During the Civil War he organized the economy to give the fullest backing possible to the Red Army, bringing in War Communism as a necessity in a dire situation. Once the Civil War was over, prompted by increasing unrest and the Kronstadt rising of 1921, he brought in the New Economic Policy to deal with the devastation and dislocation caused by the fighting. The NEP restored Russia to its pre-First World War economic position within five or six years.

Lenin is an extremely controversial figure and opinions of him vary widely, according to one's view of what he was trying to achieve and the way he went about it. Those who are critical of him can point to the fact that it was he who, in leading the Bolsheviks to power, prevented Russia from developing along Western lines with a capitalist economy and a parliamentary democracy ensuring broad freedoms for the individual. He can be seen as the founder of a dictatorship, which was harsher than the Tsar's because of its efficiency. On the other hand, one can maintain that the Communists had the very reasonable aims of creating equality and of ending a class-based society, not through giving freedoms but through property redistribution. One cannot expect a peasant society, with a tradition of backwardness and dictatorship, to be transformed overnight into a model democratic state, especially as the enemies of Bolshevism along with outside powers chose to plunge Russia into further war.

Even Lenin's sympathizers dispute the wisdom of some of his policies. Some see the NEP as a sensible move allowing for recovery, the policy of a flexible leader prepared to face realities. Others see it as a retreat to capitalism, which later had to be reversed with added complications. It is questionable whether the very narrow dictatorship, the banning of all other parties — even those with similar aims to those of the Communists — was necessary in 1921. Similarly, the outlawing of opposition groups within the party itself, and the increasing domination of the higher officials, can be considered unhealthy developments, especially in the light of the uses to which they were later put. It is ironic that, in his final years, Lenin was increasingly worried about the remoteness of the government from the people, while at the same time he was pursuing policies which accelerated this trend.

Firm conclusions are not easy to reach. Although Lenin was responsible (as far as one individual can be judged to be so) for the vast changes that took place in Russia from 1917 to 1924, he did not live to see more than the first steps taken along the way to communism. It is interesting to speculate on what policies he might have adopted had he lived to lead Russia for another 20 years. Most historians agree that Lenin was a kind person, helping friends and individuals where he could. For example, he distributed presents of food he received. He lived, despite his exalted position, in simple surroundings and he lacked personal ambition. He would not have liked the hero-worship that followed his death, nor the embalming of his body to preserve it from decay. He was motivated by a cause, and in pursuing that cause he was determined, harsh, and ruthless to anyone who stood in its way.

4

Stalin's Russia (I) — The Transformation of a Country

(1) The Struggle for the Leadership and the Triumph of Stalin

Joseph Stalin's early life Joseph Vissarionovich Djugashvili was born of serf origin in 1879, the son of a shoemaker in Georgia. At the age of 15 he entered the Theological Seminary at Tiflis to train to be a priest. He soon became involved with revolutionary ideas and read books which were not allowed by the college. This led to his expulsion from the college and thereafter Stalin became a full-time revolutionary in the Caucasus region. Before long he had become a major figure in the revolutionary politics of southern Russia. Although he had little contact with the leaders of the Russian Marxists, he nevertheless came to their attention. Stalin had little in common with the middle-class intellectuals, with their international outlook, who spent much of their time outside Russia; he remained essentially Russian. Most of his years before 1917 were spent in prison or avoiding capture. He changed his name several times, adopting Stalin, which meant 'Man of Steel', in 1913. His hard work for the Bolsheviks, which included organizing bank raids for party funds, was rewarded with the editorship of the party newspaper *Pravda* ('The Truth'), in 1912. For three weeks after the February revolution of 1917 he acted as the Bolshevik leader, but retreated to the wings on Lenin's return. He remained a relatively unknown figure, and was therefore not arrested after the July Days, although he was an active supporter of Lenin. When the Bolsheviks seized power in October 1917 he was given the post of

1917 — Commissar for the Nationalities Commissar for the Nationalities, as a result of an article he had previously written on this subject. He was now responsible for the affairs of the 65 million non-Russian peoples in the Soviet state. The detailed knowledge of their customs and traditions that he obtained gave him an unchallenged authority in this field. It was in this post that he ordered Georgian independence to be crushed in 1921.

The party organizer Stalin was not a brilliant intellectual, full of original ideas, nor was he an inspiring speaker. He was above all a hard-working administrator, prepared to do the grind that more capable government members found tedious. The Communist Party was now the party of government. It was no longer the focus of organized revolutionary opposition, and of necessity it became more complex. It needed someone to organize its affairs and to co-ordinate its activities throughout the country. Stalin's particular abilities and his membership of the inner cabinet of the party, the Politburo, made him the natural choice as party organizer. The Organizational Bureau, the Orgburo, increasingly became his domain. He managed day-to-day matters and directed party personnel where they were needed.

Stalin (centre) as General Secretary of the Communist Party of the Soviet Union, 1929

1922 — General
Secretary

His success in this field led to his appointment as head of the Commissariat (*Rabkrin*) established in 1919 to make sure that government functioned fairly and efficiently. It had considerable powers of inspection in all government departments, was expected to train reliable civil servants for government posts, and, under Stalin, came to control virtually the whole machinery of government. A similar body set up to supervise the party soon came into his hands and, in 1922, he also became the party's first General Secretary. Although often out of the limelight he slowly established control of the government and party machinery, by appointing people whom he trusted and who looked up to him.

Lenin attempts
to remove him

Lenin was one of the few to realize just how much power Stalin had gathered. Ill-health prevented him from taking action (see p. 38) and during the months of Lenin's enforced absence from state affairs, Stalin moved carefully. He made sure that he appeared as a moderate figure, humble, loyal to Lenin and the party and unambitious. He accepted criticisms and proposed corrections. Few considered him as a possible successor to Lenin; after all, he lacked the obvious qualities of leadership. He was variously described as 'the arch mediocrity of our party' (Trotsky) and as a figure that 'produced . . . the impression of a grey blur' (Sukhanov).

Trotsky out-
manoeuvred

The most likely new leader was Leon Trotsky, a man of recognized brilliance, yet one whose arrogance and obvious contempt for so many had cost him much personal support. He was the one man people imagined might be planning a take-over. Parallels with the French Revolution were continually in people's minds and many saw Trotsky as the potential Napoleon, who would take advantage of the uncertainties of the situation to establish himself as a dictator with the support of the Red Army. Therefore, as Lenin lay dying, there was opposition to Trotsky and a leadership of three — a triumvirate — was established. Its members were Stalin, Kamenev and Zinoviev. The last two were both close associates of Lenin. Kamenev was Party Secretary in Moscow, while Zinoviev was Party Secretary in Petrograd as well as Chairman of Comintern. Stalin was an invaluable colleague. With his influence over the party membership he was able to command majority votes at party congresses. An attack on the triumvirate and the party bureaucracy by Trotsky and his supporters was easily smothered by Stalin in this way.

If Trotsky is to be believed, Stalin did not inform him of the date of Lenin's funeral and because he was out of Moscow, recovering from an illness, he missed it. Stalin, in particular, played a large part in the funeral and in the tributes, and he was now continually in the public eye. The greatest danger to him was the possible publication of Lenin's will and testament which called for his removal. Krupskaya, Lenin's widow, sent it to the Central Committee of the party with a view to having it read before the next party Congress. However, when it was presented, Zinoviev and Kamenev put in a good word for Stalin and the proposal for publication was defeated by 30 votes to 10.

Stalin v.
Trotsky

Stalin's quarrel with Trotsky was mainly one of personality and they had clashed several times earlier in their careers. He now did all he could to discredit Trotsky, although he left Zinoviev and Kamenev to lead the attack. Trotsky gave as good as he got and all three were brought into disrepute in the process, as previous disagreements with Lenin were brought into the open. But Stalin and Trotsky also had very different views on the priorities for the development of Russia into a Socialist state. Trotsky believed in

'Permanent
Revolution'

'permanent revolution'; that Russia would not develop fully into a Socialist state without revolution occurring elsewhere in Europe. He argued that Russia would probably be crushed by the capitalist powers before she had a chance to build herself up and that it would be very difficult for backward Russia to industrialize without aid from other more advanced states. His

'Socialism in
one Country'

priority was therefore to spread the revolution beyond Russia's borders. Stalin, however, coined a new phrase, 'Socialism in One Country'. He claimed that Russia had the resources to industrialize and develop a Socialist society, although he did not explain how this could be done. Russia must build herself up first and then the revolution would spread elsewhere. Stalin's 'Socialism in One Country' proved the more popular policy with many Russians because, at this stage, it appeared the more optimistic; nor did it depend on revolutions occurring elsewhere, which were looking increasingly unlikely anyway. It seemed to point the way to stability and increasing prosperity, rather than to plunge Russia into another period of upheaval and self-sacrifice. It was officially adopted at the 14th Party

Congress in 1925.

By this time Trotsky had been eased out of his leadership of the Red Army, where he had his main support. He did not attempt to save himself, as he was not prepared to use general discontent in the country against the party and he could not win the party vote while Stalin was General Secretary. Having thus virtually disposed of Trotsky, Stalin now broke with Zinoviev and Kamenev, using economic policy debates to do so. He managed to isolate them from the other members of the Politburo with the aid of the right wing of the party, led by Bukharin. They realized too late what Stalin was up to, so they turned to Trotsky, and tried to organize a workers' revolt against the government on the tenth anniversary of the Revolution. For this they were expelled from the party and were only

Trotsky
deported

allowed back on full admission of guilt. By 1928 they were no longer a threat to Stalin, and in the same year Trotsky was exiled to Alma Ata in Central Asia. In 1929 he was deported from Russia on Stalin's orders. Stalin then attacked the policies of Bukharin and the right wing of the party. He argued that their policies would lead to the restoration of capitalism, and as a result the group was publicly forced to renounce its views.

Stalin
triumphant

Stalin had gradually used the different personalities and viewpoints within the party to isolate and humiliate all his potential rivals. As Bukharin had once whispered to Kamenev:

> He is an unprincipled intriguer who subordinates everything to his appetite for power. At any given moment he will change his theories in order to get rid of someone.

At the end of 1929 Stalin was 50. No doubt he enjoyed his birthday with a certain feeling of smug satisfaction. The 'arch-mediocrity' had outwitted all his rivals.

(2) The Soviet Economy and the Future

The limitations
of NEP

The organization of the Soviet economy in the 1920s was a compromise between full state control and a return to capitalism. NEP had been introduced to provide a breathing space and a chance to recover from the depths of 1921–2. By 1925–6 pre-war levels had pretty well been reached in agricultural production, and small businesses had revived; but large-scale industry was still well behind its 1913 production figures. There were also some basic economic problems which had not been solved. The main one was how to get the farmers to sell sufficient produce to the towns, while industry was producing too few goods at too high a price for them to buy with the money they might make. In 1925–6 the government tried to encourage the richer peasants, the kulaks, who usually had surplus produce to sell, by cutting their taxes and by lessening the restrictions on hiring labour, but this did not overcome the problem of the lack of goods for them to buy.

Full
industrialization
policy

With basic recovery achieved the party now voted for a policy of industrial development on a large scale. It was time to see Russia progress from her backward state. Industrialization would bring national strength, so vital in a hostile capitalist world. In the long run it would also bring improved living standards and make possible the building of a socialist and later communist state, where the mass of people were industrial workers not peasants. Certain interrelated questions had to be answered first. Which industries should they concentrate on? How quickly should the industrialization take place? How was the development to be financed?

Priority on   It was decided to go first for the development of heavy industry, for what
heavy industry are known as capital goods, those which are used to produce other goods, e.g. iron and steel, machine tools, electric power, transport. These would provide the industrial base not only for future development but also for military power. Consumer goods, which people might use to make life more comfortable and which might have encouraged the kulaks to sell more food to help finance the industrial development, would not do much for Russia's strength. It was decided that their manufacture would have to be postponed.

Industry in Russia in the 1920s

Problems of   The other two questions were intertwined, for the speed of the develop-
financing   ment would inevitably depend greatly on the finances available. Originally
industry   the party had hoped that financial aid would come from an industrially-developed socialist state, probably Germany, once the revolution had spread. Now that this had failed to happen, and Russia had recognized the fact in adopting Stalin's policy of 'Socialism in One Country', Russia was dependent on her own resources. Money to finance development would have to come mainly from agriculture. More food would have to be grown

and sold, and much of it exported to buy the foreign technology that Russia lacked. It would have to be grown by fewer people, so that the extra labour could be released to form the new industrial workforce. The production of more food was in itself a major problem, for Russian agriculture was basically inefficient and backward. Too many farms were run on medieval lines, such as strip farming and field rotation, with out-of-date equipment. Large units tend to be more efficient in their use of man-power, machinery, and marketing; they make more money with which to buy necessary machinery; larger units can experiment with new farming ideas, which are impossible for the small farmer growing just enough for his own needs. Yet Russian agriculture was based on the small farmer, and the number of peasant owners had been increased by no less than seven million by the government's policy of land distribution in 1917.

Collective farm policy

There were two ways of dealing with the problem. The first was to encourage the kulaks to grow more and to buy out the small farmer. The kulaks would be rewarded with a good return for their produce. But this would encourage private initiative on a large scale — in other words restore capitalism — and so it was hardly an attractive policy for the Communist Party. Anyway, urban industry would still not be producing goods the kulaks would wish to buy. The second alternative was to form collective farms. In these the land and equipment of the individual farmers would be pooled to form a large-scale unit, with a greater potential for efficiency and increased production. Clearly, this was the more attractive solution to the party, but it was unlikely to be popular with the peasantry. The better-off at least were hardly likely to want to pool their land and equipment. Force at this stage was ruled out and instead a policy of gradual collectivization of the land was adopted. Yet at the same time the party voted for a policy of rapid industrialization, despite fears that this was unrealistic and would not be achieved without massive upheaval and great hardship for the Russian people.

Debates on the economy were widespread and relatively free, for at that stage there was no definite party line. But they provided a setting for the personal rivalry and power struggle that was taking place in the mid-'20s. For example, Stalin sided with Bukharin against Trotsky's plans for rapid industrialization in 1925; yet once Trotsky was out of the way he changed his mind and turned on the Bukharin faction for being too favourable to the kulaks.

From 1926 the party and government were committed to rapid industrialization and planning discussions began, centred on the state planning authority, Gosplan. While strategy and production targets were being decided some schemes were started without delay. These included the Dnieper Dam hydro-electric scheme to provide the new industries with power; the Stalingrad tractor plant to provide vital agricultural machinery; and the Turksib (Turkestan-Siberia) railway to carry grain from Siberia to

The End of NEP and First Five-Year Plan(1928)

cotton-growing Central Asia. The full-scale plans were ready by 1928. NEP came to an end and Russia entered her First Five-Year Plan (1928–33) with a most ambitious programme of state-controlled industrial and agricultural development. The figures were approved by the Party Congress in April 1929, by which time the plan was already in operation. The targets were an overall increase in industrial production of 180%, including a 335%

Rapid industrialisation — five-year plan in four years ('2 + 2 and the enthusiasm of the workers = 5)

increase in electric power, a 200% increase in iron production, and a 111% increase in coal.

Such figures seemed highly unrealistic; yet enthusiasts were soon proclaiming the target of 'The Five-Year Plan in Four Years'. By 1931 Stalin was talking in terms of fulfilling the plan in three years 'in all the basic, decisive, branches of industry'. It was to be an economic miracle with state rather than divine intervention! It would see Russia transformed from an agrarian society, whose feet had been in the Middle Ages, to one 'advancing full steam ahead along the path of industrialization to socialism, leaving behind the age-long Russian backwardness' (Stalin, 1929). The Russian leaders were very conscious of the economic and military might of the developed capitalist world, and of Russia's need to catch up. In a speech in February 1931 Stalin reminded his audience that

> those who are backward are beaten. . . . We are 50 to 100 years behind the advanced countries. We must make up this gap in 10 years. Either we do this, or they crush us.

The economic plans therefore concentrated on heavy industries: on iron, coal, steel, oil, chemicals, and machine production, and in comparison neglected consumer goods. Making life more pleasant for the average Russian would have to be left to a later date.

(3) The Collectivization of Agriculture

The target set for increased agricultural production under the First Five-Year Plan was 55%, and it was estimated that 15% of farm produce would be coming from collectives by 1932. It was still assumed in early 1928 that collectivization would be carried out 'gradually but surely, not by pressure but by example and persuasion'. During that year, however, Stalin's (and Collectivization therefore the party's) policy became one of rapid collectivization at all costs. at all costs The change came like a bolt out of the blue.

The most obvious cause was the continuing failure of the agricultural sector of the economy to produce the grain for the towns, even when harvests were good. The amount the government received at the fixed state prices in 1927 was half that of the previous year and at least two million tons short of what was considered necessary. The farmers preferred to sell to private traders from whom they received a higher price. Stalin's answer was to revert to something similar to the grain seizures of War Communism. He himself went to the Urals-Siberia area to organize the forcible seizure of grain from the richer peasants, the kulaks, and the closing of the private markets. Other top party officials were sent elsewhere to organize similar campaigns against 'hoarders' and 'speculators'. Despite this example, or perhaps because of it, the situation of 1928–9 was even worse and the amount of grain available for the towns would have reduced them to near starvation. This was indeed a far cry from surplus agricultural production helping to finance rapid industrialization.

In November 1929 Stalin announced that collectivization would proceed apace. He even claimed that the middle and poor peasants were already seeing its benefits and were moving into collectives. How far pressure had been brought to bear is impossible to say. Stalin was totally unsympathetic to the peasantry and their continual failure to see beyond their own immediate gain. He was not prepared to try to win them round gradually to War on the his ideas. Instead he declared war on the kulaks and proposed their kulaks destruction. 'Now we are able to carry on a determined offensive against the kulaks, and to eliminate them as a class', he announced in December 1929. Kulaks were not even to be allowed to join the new collectives for they were class enemies and would attempt to sabotage them. Instead their land, animals, and equipment were seized to join with that of the other peasants and most of them were deported to regions far away. Any farmers showing active hostility were dealt with by the secret police, being shot or sent to labour camps. A few were allowed to remain in their local area, but on land which would not give them a living. Party agents, backed up by the police, now organized the new collective farms. Despite the added resources of the kulaks, however, the majority of the other peasants did not welcome the

Violent scheme and mounted resistance. A sort of civil war broke out in some areas.
opposition to Rather than share their land and animals, peasants began to destroy their
collectivization property and to slaughter their livestock on a huge scale. The upheaval in the countryside was tremendous, yet Stalin was able to claim that 50% of the peasants had joined collectives by February 1930. But the harvest of 1930 was obviously in danger. In a speech that March, Stalin called a temporary halt, alleging that certain officials had been over-keen and had allowed their enthusiasm to carry them away into using excessive force: they were 'dizzy with success'. He announced that the peasants should keep possession of their houses, gardens, orchards, and some of their animals. He continued the myth that the collective movement was voluntary and the result was that in a few months the percentage of households in collectives dropped from

The policy 57·6 to 23·6, as whole areas abandoned them. Pressure was then re-applied
enforced and by 1935 94% of the crop area and 83% of farm households had been brought into collectives. The opposition remained violent, the destruction of livestock enormous. Between 1929 and 1933 53% of horses, 45% of cattle,
Destruction of and 67% of sheep and goats were lost. Farm output slumped and the amount
livestock the state could buy was badly affected. The peasants, however, were fighting a losing battle. Stalin remained determined to carry out his policy. He made sure that the industrial workers got what they needed from the farm produce available. The death penalty was introduced for pilfering or destroying the produce of a collective; in special circumstances this could be reduced to 10 years hard labour and loss of all one's property. It was to be the peasantry who paid the price of change. Although it was not officially admitted at the
Famine, 1933 time, large areas were at starvation level in 1933. During this time 10 million people remain unaccounted for — they probably starved. Stories of cannibalism appeared, of desperate peasants carving up strangers or even their own children for meat.

	1928	1930	1932
Total grain production (million tons)	73·3	83·5	69·6
State purchase	10·8	22·1	18·5

Once opposition had been revealed as futile and the policy enforced, production began to rise again slowly. Production figures gradually climbed from the low point of 1933, though they remained disappointing. In 1937, in very good weather, there was a record harvest of 97·4 million tons of grain. Livestock numbers gradually recovered. On the government side the attitude eased slightly. It was officially declared in 1935 that the peasants

Private plots
allowed

were to be allowed to keep their private plots (of a maximum area of 0·5 hectares), one cow, two calves, one sow, 10 sheep or goats, and an unlimited number of poultry and rabbits.

The *kolkhoz*

The typical unit of agricultural production was now the *kolkhoz* (collective), in which an average 75 households surrendered private ownership of their land and most of their animals to the state, and farmed together. The state demanded a certain percentage of their produce at a fixed low price and the rest was then divided among the workers as pay. This was done according to the amount of work done, rather than the initial amount of land put in, and even then it was based on 'work days' whereby skilled work was more highly rewarded. Any surplus remaining after pay was sold and the profits shared. Each household was required to work a set number of days, say 100 to 150 each year, on the communal lands. The rest could be spent on their own plot and they were allowed to sell any of their produce privately at market. It became a widely known, if somewhat disguised, fact of life that the peasants usually worked harder on their own land than on the collective's. The private plot produced most of the fruit and vegetables, meat, milk and eggs and was a major source of income for most families. The *kolkhozes* were run by elected officials and committees, and the top officials were usually party men. There were also state farms where the land was owned by the state and the workers were paid for the work they did. These had the advantage for the government of producing food which was then theirs to dispose of; but, on the other hand, there was a fixed outlay on wages, which had to be paid whether the harvest was good or not.

State farms

Machine tractor
stations (MTS)

Russian farmers were accustomed to using very simple tools and little machinery. One way of increasing efficiency was to introduce tractors and more modern equipment. In 1928 the government set up machine tractor stations (MTS) across the country. These loaned the necessary machinery to the collectives and provided trained personnel to operate and service it, since most peasants had no idea how to use it. Payment was in produce, which gave the state additional food supplies. In the early days of collectivization political agents were also based on the MTS to keep an eye on the Russian farmers. By 1935 there were 4375 such stations, and by 1940 this had risen to 7069.

(4) Industry and Labour

The labour
force; volun-
teers and
conscripts

At the same time as the collectivization of agriculture was being implemented, huge new industrial projects were under way, not only in the already somewhat industrialized areas of western and southern Russia, but also in central Asia, Kazakhstan, and Georgia. Planning and human effort on a vast scale were required, and there was massive state intervention in an attempt to direct labour and resources to where they were needed most. Many thousands of enthusiastic volunteers made their way to remote regions to undertake the building of a new steelworks or dam, inspired by the challenge of developing their country. Where these volunteers were insufficient, labour was drafted; in this decade there were always plenty of prisoners who could be sent to the least hospitable areas of Russia to slave under armed guard on new projects. Labour presented an immense problem in the country as a whole. Backward peasants lacked the skills necessary for industry, and the labour force was highly unstable. People on average changed their job about three times every two years, so there was little chance to learn even basic skills. There was certainly little incentive to stay put: wages were low, housing often lacked basic sanitation, and accommodation was insufficient for the huge numbers involved. A survey in Moscow in 1935 revealed that only 6% of households had more than one room, and nearly 25% shared a room. Food and consumer goods were in short supply and rationing had to be introduced. Prices rose faster than wages and there was a marked drop in living standards, despite Stalin's claim that 'the material conditions of the workers and peasants are improving from year to year'. This statement was made in 1933, the year of the great famine in the countryside, a year which saw 'the culmination of the most precipitous peacetime decline in living standards known in recorded history'*. In view of this situation the government introduced internal passports in December 1932 to check movement, and tightened up discipline at work. One day's absence without sufficient reason could lead to dismissal together with a loss of housing and food cards. Targets for production were publicized and individual factories and work units were encouraged to reach or surpass their target figures. The trade unions had their role to play, not in the traditional way of protecting their workers, but rather as the link between government and worker, getting the highest possible production from their members. 'Socialist competition' between factories and areas to achieve the highest output was emphasized. Sometimes managers and statisticians were keener to meet their schedules than they were to make sure that quality was maintained. A factory could turn out a record area of glass, but it might be too thin to use!

By 1932 the official statistics showed that the overall targets of the First Five-Year Plan had been reached. But these figures were based on money values rather than volume of production. They were therefore distorted as money had lost much of its value. In volume of goods nearly every sector of the economy failed to reach its target; yet this is not to deny the very real advances that had been made. Coal production was up 80% on its 1927–8 level, pig iron production 100%, electricity output was up 160% and the number of industrial workers had increased by 100%. A huge new power station on the Dnieper River had also been opened.

Immediately a Second Five-Year Plan for the years 1932–7 was launched. This was again highly unrealistic and had to be revised two years later to a more sensible level. The economy was overstrained, and year after year of rapid growth was simply not possible until certain factors had been dealt with. For example, the transport system was totally inadequate to meet the needs of industry, while the dislocation in the countryside in 1933–4 affected the rate of increase possible in industry. Nevertheless, during the period of industrialization the government did all it could to encourage high output. Skilled workers were considered more valuable than manual labourers and were rewarded with higher wages, holidays, and honours. The communist ideal of equal wages for everyone was looked down upon by Stalin as

Poor living standards (margin note)

The Second Five-Year Plan (margin note)

* A. Nove; *An Economic History of the USSR* (Pelican edition, 1972; p. 207)

The
'Stakhanovites'
'levelling'. In 1935 Alexei Stakhanov, a coal miner, cut 102 tons of coal in a six-hour shift (an output 14 times the normal), and he soon became a national hero, giving his name to the Stakhanovite movement of skilled workers. Everyone was now expected to produce similar quantities, even if they lacked the assistance and modern equipment which facilitated the unexpectedly high output. Wage levels were fixed according to the levels obtained by the Stakhanovites and output below this meant lower wages. Despite this, real wages for the urban worker did rise by over a third during the Second Plan and, by 1937, they were about 80% of the 1928 level. Labour discipline, however, was made even tighter. By 1938 each worker had a work-book in which his work record was entered, including such 'crimes' as absence for no good reason, and without this book he could not get a job.

The results of the Second Five-Year Plan were staggering. Coal production had doubled again since 1932, steel production had trebled, electric power production showed very nearly a similar increase and there had even been expansion in some goods useful to the Russian people, such as cloth and shoes. The number of machine tools produced had trebled; Russia was now only importing 10% of her machinery, whereas during the First Plan she had imported 78%. Many projects had been completed: for example, a huge metal-producing complex in the Urals–Kutznetsk region, and a massive steelworks at Magnitogorsk. Many of the developments were in the formerly less developed Asiatic parts of Russia, where mineral deposits were exploited for the first time. As well as opening up these backward areas, the developments had strategic importance, for they were less vulnerable to external attack than western Russia and were to prove their worth during the Second World War. Transport, too, had been improved. Many new railway lines had been opened and single lines made double; the rail-freight carried had nearly doubled since 1932. Major highways had been built and air services to remoter regions established. Two huge waterway projects, the Baltic-White Sea canal and the Moscow-Volga canal linked industrially important areas and cut water transport distances. Moscow had become a major river port.

The Third Five-
Year Plan
The Third Plan, launched in 1938, predicted further expansion and an increasing number of consumer goods. Despite the effect of the purges on industry (p. 58), some progress was made, but the increasingly dangerous international situation meant a change in priorities, and the plan came to concentrate very heavily on defence expenditure. One quarter of the 1939 national budget went on this sector. By 1940 a war economy had developed and workers were not allowed to leave their jobs without official permission. The final blow to progress came with the German invasion in the summer of 1941.

5
Stalin's Russia (II)

(1) Education, the Family, and the Arts

Advances in
educational
provision

The Bolsheviks always had free compulsory education as a major aim and in the 1920s did much to realize this, at least in the field of primary schooling. A major campaign was launched against the widespread illiteracy, and adult education classes for workers beyond school age were set up. At the same time there was a revulsion against traditional education, with its strict discipline and emphasis on examination marks. Higher education was thrown open to all who wished to participate, no matter what their academic standard. But the developing industrial society of the 1930s required advanced technical expertise, scientific knowledge and a skilled labour force. So the Five-Year Plans made great strides in improving the availability and quality of all sectors of education, with a special emphasis on science and technology. During the First Plan alone the numbers attending secondary schools trebled to over two million pupils. By the end of the 1930s

Peasants in Soviet Russia being taught to write

illiteracy had been reduced to about 15% of the population, and most of these were the old people. By 1941 there were nearly a million graduates working in the economy. The number of medical students increased too, and the number of doctors rose from 70 000 in 1928 to 155 000 in 1940; many were women. Medical care improved greatly as did the number of hospital beds available, and the government spent large sums on social security and social insurance.

Experimentation dropped The experimentation that had taken place in education during the 1920s was dropped and a more formal system introduced — academic learning, obedience, and high examination marks were once again stressed. Higher education was restricted to those with 10 years of secondary education and the necessary examination passes. It was also normally limited to the politically 'safe' and to members of the Communist Youth Organization, *Komsomol.* The authorities were well aware of the role of education in furthering the Marxist cause, and political education formed part of the curriculum. From 1934 history teaching, which had been abolished, was **The uses of history . . .** reintroduced and the history textbooks were rewritten several times until they exactly suited Stalin's taste. Stalin himself was given a most prominent part in the revolution of 1917 as Lenin's right-hand man, a position he had in no way occupied. Trotsky was written out, except as a cause of all Russia's troubles since that date. In the history textbooks, and in general, patriotism **. . . and patriotism** again became respectable, rather than despised as 'bourgeois nationalism'. This was perhaps a natural consequence of the doctrine of 'Socialism in One Country' and the failure of international revolution. It certainly inspired people to greater efforts in building up Russia. Typical of the new feeling are a few lines from the official newspaper *Pravda* in 1936. 'We workers of the Soviet Union love our fatherland. We are patriots . . . even the air of the Soviets is holy to us.' Selected Tsars, such as Ivan the Terrible and Peter the Great, who had strengthened or modernized Russia, became national heroes rather than Tsarist tyrants. Events, such as the retreat of Napoleon from Russia in 1812, were again remembered with pride.

The family Other traditional features of Russian life regained their former officially respected place. The institution of the family, which had been somewhat undermined by the early revolutionaries as a conservative force, recovered its place at the centre of Russian life. Divorce and abortion, readily available after 1917, were now more difficult to obtain. Two major problems prompted this change of policy — the declining birthrate and the increase in juvenile delinquency. Large families were encouraged by financial incentives, such as tax reductions; titles, such as 'Mothers' Heroine' for a woman who reared 10 children, were awarded. On the other hand, families became collectively responsible for the actions of one member: a treasonable act by one could lead to punishment for all. Also, youngsters over the age of 12 became criminally responsible, liable, at worst, to the death sentence.

The arts Literature and the arts had suffered greatly from the emigration of many of Russia's most celebrated figures during the revolution, and also from the communist wish to use the arts as a means of educating the people to socialism. The period of the NEP had been relatively free and many works of value had been produced. But after the introduction of the Five-Year Plans the arts became the servants of the state, and artists and writers were

'Socialist
Realism'
expected to produce works of 'Socialist Realism', conforming to the correct political viewpoint on topics suitable for the first workers' state. Works on the noble idealism of collective farmers and Stakhanovites became the order of the day, and only members of the official 'Writers Union' could have their works published. Stalin's daughter, Svetlana, said that the man in charge of the policy, Zhdanov, 'viewed art from the bigoted and puritanical point of view prevalent in the party'. A cultural wilderness was created by men who had no real knowledge of the field and who saw the expression of individual creativity as a threat to existing values and order. The writer whose words were quoted most often and whose style was the most admired, was Joseph Stalin.

(2) The Purges, the Show Trials, and the 1936 Constitution

During the period of rapid change, of collectivization and war on the kulaks, of industrialization at break-neck speed, of sacrifice and of upheaval, Stalin and his secret police — now known as OGPU — kept a close watch on any potential opponents of the regime or its plans. Anyone who could possibly be regarded as a wrecker or saboteur was rooted out and severely dealt with. Throughout the years of the First Five-Year Plan people suspected of trying to hinder progress were arrested and tried. Many were accused of conspiring with foreign powers, some even of planning to kill Stalin and the other leaders. Long prison sentences were handed out. As violence in the country-side grew, especially against collectivization, and as starvation threatened, opposition to Stalin's policies was increasingly expressed among circles close to and within the government. The arrest and deportation of thousands followed and purges of party members became a common feature in provinces where government policies met hostility. In the Ukraine for example, 28 000 party members were expelled and 237 Party Secretaries dismissed in 1933.

Stalin's wife's
suicide
Only once in his vendetta against opposition did Stalin appear to lose his nerve. In November 1932 Nadezhda Alliluyeva, Stalin's second wife, expressed her doubts, in company, about the terror policies of the government. Stalin turned on her and after an unpleasant scene she left; she committed suicide that night. Stalin even offered to resign, but the offer was quickly brushed over by an embarrassed Politburo, and the 'man of steel's' nerve soon recovered. He remained extremely wary of any criticism, of any suggested alteration of his policies, and above all of any potential rivals for his position as leader. One such man was Sergei Kirov, the party leader in Leningrad who had been a member of the Politburo since 1930. He was young, good looking, popular and known to be more moderate in his
Kirov's murder economic policies than Stalin. On 1 December 1934 he was shot dead in his office. The circumstances were suspicious, and they were made more so by the death in a car accident shortly afterwards of a key witness on his way to give evidence; other people in the car were unharmed. Was Stalin responsible or was he simply frightened by the murder? We shall probably never know for sure. What we do know is that the Kirov murder set off a period of blood-letting and terror on an incredible scale, as Stalin lashed out in all directions to cut down and remove every potential enemy.

The 'Show Trials'

The months directly following the murder witnessed frenzied activity by the Internal Affairs Commisariat (the NKVD) in which OGPU had been merged. Thousands were deported on suspicion alone and hundreds were executed. The party was purged of vast numbers; in fact, in the four years 1933–7 over one million people were expelled. Devoted life service to the party, and a part in the 1917 Revolution did not remove one from suspicion; quite the reverse. All the members of Lenin's Politburo, except for Stalin and Trotsky, ended up on trial. So, too, did many of Stalin's other former associates, accused of the most outrageous crimes — of trying to wreck the Soviet economy, of wishing to restore capitalism, of plotting to kill Stalin. Many were supposedly in collaboration with the exiled Trotsky or with the capitalist powers, even with Adolf Hitler, the arch-enemy of communism.

A resolution denouncing the accused in one of the show trials being read in a factory in 1938

Many secret trials followed, but there were also public ones, often of the best-known figures. The most famous trials were those of 'the Sixteen' in August 1936, of 'the Seventeen' in January 1937, and of 'the Twenty-one' in March 1938. They brought into the dock such famous former leaders as Zinoviev, Kamenev, Bukharin and Rykov, and in the last major trial in 1938 the former head of the secret police, Yagoda, who had provided the evidence against those accused earlier. The cases were given great publicity and they became known as the 'Show Trials'. Perhaps the most amazing feature of the whole proceedings was the public confession of guilt of so many of the

Public confessions

accused. They willingly, it appeared, confessed to crimes they could not have committed, knowing full well that the outcome would be execution. Some seemed so keen to add to their crimes that they had to be told to shut up and were made to stand down. They had obviously been 'softened up' by threats to their families and by torture. Some of the accused had the strength to withstand hours, even days, of continual interrogation under bright lights; some stood up to being beaten, to having fingers crushed in the door, even to being put in the wet punishment cell where they were left with water up to their knees. For them, secret trials away from the glare of publicity were necessary. Others confessed because they realised the hopelessness of the situation, or because they were loyal Communists and did not wish to bring the party and the first Communist state into disrepute by revealing the horrible charade that was taking place. Some members of the party's Central Committee spoke out against what was going on, only to find themselves on trial as accessories and sentenced to death.

Army purges   In some of the early trials 'evidence' was produced implicating the army, and in 1937 a secret trial of Russia's top soldier, Marshal Tukhachevsky, and seven generals took place. Being found guilty of conspiring with Germany and Japan they were shot and before long over half the officer corps, about 35 000 men, had been removed — many were sentenced to death or long periods of penal servitude. Coming at a time of increasing international tension this purge seriously weakened the Russian military build-up.

Terror   No section of Russian society was safe from the onslaught. The mid-1930s was a time of suspicion and terror, of neighbours denouncing former friends, of the dreaded arrival of the police in the middle of the night to arrest family members. People disappeared without trace. Many business managers and members of the intelligentsia, such as writers and professors, were among the victims. The Church continued to be harassed and 40 bishops were among those executed. The number of people involved is impossible to assess; conservative estimates suggest 7 or 8 million, others say as many as 23 million.

Promotions   With so many people being removed others were rapidly promoted. In the party and government, people who had regarded Stalin as their equal or even their inferior, or who had played a prominent part in the 1917 Revolution, were replaced by men who looked up to Stalin and were 'his' men: people like Nikita Khrushchev, who now became Secretary of the Moscow Party Organization; Georgi Malenkov, later Stalin's choice as his successor; and Lavrentii Beria, who rose to be head of the NKVD. In lesser jobs the new appointees tended to be against change; they were good at carrying out orders rather than bringing in new ideas. The effect of the purges was felt in business too, as people were scared to show too much initiative or to take responsibility, lest their plans failed or their inventiveness was taken as a threat to the existing situation and their superiors.

In 1938 Stalin at last called a halt, purged the NKVD officers who had been in charge of the arrests and trials, and even freed and rehabilitated some of the people found guilty. He had no fears now of rivals. The nation was firmly under his control. The danger that in some future war he might be removed, like the Tsar in the last one, now seemed remote. Stalin emerged with his reputation largely intact, for the terror was blamed on his officials rather than on Stalin himself who had in fact instigated it. During the 1930s, government propaganda continued to present Stalin as a kind man, a wise leader, a devoted follower of Lenin who, with the aid of his loyal supporters and citizens, was transforming Russia into a modern world power.

The murder of   One final blow remained to be struck. The man most often accused during Trotsky   the trials had so far evaded 'justice'. Trotsky, driven into exile, was now living in Mexico, where he spent much of his time writing attacks on Stalin. But in August 1940 one of Stalin's agents caught up with him and smashed his head open with an ice axe — his blood splattered over the page of a biography of Joseph Stalin he was writing.

In the midst of the purges came a new constitution for the Soviet Union. The 1924 system of government was considered to be in need of revision to reflect the changes in society that had taken place since then. In a blaze of publicity, recommendations were put, discussed, and adopted finally in December 1936. The new 'Stalin Constitution' defined the USSR as a socialist state with 'socialist ownership of the instruments and means of production' operating on the principle of 'from each according to his ability, to each according to his work'. The withering away of the state, which communism predicted should now take place, was unfortunately not possible because of the encirclement of the USSR by hostile capitalist powers. Instead the Constitution laid down the structure of government for the near future. Everyone over the age of 18, no matter what his class background, was now allowed to vote every four years for a Parliament or Supreme Soviet in which all legal authority rested. This unwieldy body of nearly 1400 members met only irregularly. It vested its powers in a Presidium and a Council of Ministers to carry out its functions and to run the government.

The Constitution also recognized the rights of the people to work, to leisure, to education, to free medical care and to liberties such as freedom of speech, freedom of the press and freedom from unlawful arrest. These freedoms were, however, to be 'in conformity with the interests of the working people' — a phrase which could obviously be interpreted to mean almost anything. Because of the guarantee of these rights and the universal vote, Stalin proclaimed the new Constitution as 'the only thoroughly democratic constitution in the world'. As so often in Soviet life, theory and practice were, however, somewhat at variance with each other. The free elections, in reality, gave the people a chance to vote for a list of candidates selected by the Communist Party, which remained the only legal political party, 'the leading core of all organizations', and 'the vanguard of the working people'. The Communists justified this on the grounds that different political parties were only essential where different classes had conflicting interests, and as the Soviet people were all in harmony only one party was necessary. It remained a fact of Soviet life that the party had the real power and that the party leaders and the top politicians were the same people. As for the rights of the individual — perhaps it suffices to say that the year of the New Constitution was also the year in which the arrests and trials reached their peak.

(3) The 1930s — Some Conclusions

The achievements of the 1930s had been remarkable. Russia had begun its transformation from a backward agricultural nation to a modern industrial state. At a time when the Western world had been going through a severe depression, the USSR had built up a considerable industrial base. By 1939 she had overtaken the industrial output of Britain and France and was close on the heels of Germany. Whole new industrial complexes and cities had grown from nothing, and one-third of her population now lived in towns compared with one-sixth in 1926. Even her agriculture was now producing more; the area under cultivation had increased by 21%, and the number of agricultural workers per acre had been cut. One cannot help but be impressed; but one must remember the human cost of this rapid development and transformation. The peasantry had been forcibly collectivized and many of them had been deported as kulaks and class enemies. The industrial workers had been made to slave under military discipline to meet the targets of the planners. Much of the original energy and idealism for the creation of a new and better society had vanished. There was less and less room for the individual. Not only was his destiny now subject to the common cause, it was also at the mercy of one man's wish to bend the nation to his will. Some people have defended Stalin, claiming that the aim of rapidly creating an industrialized nation justified what he did. There is no such excuse for the self-glorification which he also practised. The early Communists had shied away from glorifying individuals. Stalin reversed this completely, presenting himself as some kind of demi-god. He tolerated no opposition or rival to his leadership and was prepared to go to any lengths to safeguard his position as dictator.

6
Stalin's Russia (III)

(1) Foreign Affairs 1924-33

The use of Soviet foreign policy simply to further world revolution had already been modified by the time Lenin died. Trade treaties were signed and normal diplomatic relations were established with an increasing number of countries (pp. 37-8). This tied in well with the policy of 'Socialism in One Country' adopted in the mid-1920s. The main pillar of Soviet diplomacy remained the Rapallo Treaty with Weimar Germany, renewed by a neutrality agreement in 1926. This helped Russia's efforts to keep Germany out of the Western camp where she might have become a part of an anti-Soviet alliance. It also brought German technology and machinery to Russia. So the USSR did not welcome Germany's improved relations with the West, which the Locarno treaties (1925) and German entry into the League of Nations (1926), indicated (CORE, pp. 8-9). But Soviet relations with other countries were undermined by mutual fear and suspicion. Britain provides a good example of this. Diplomatic relations were established by the first Labour Prime Minister, Ramsay Macdonald, in 1924; but they were broken off again in 1927 after a British police raid on the Anglo-Soviet Trading Organization revealed it as a centre of espionage. Relations were re-established in 1929, but they remained strained, partly as a result of Soviet attacks on British imperialism in India and the Middle East.

In Asia, the USSR continued to champion nationalist movements, in particular supporting the Chinese Nationalists (the Kuomintang) against foreign powers and warlords (AA, p. 8). The Chinese Communists were required to co-operate with the Kuomintang. But this policy received a severe setback in 1927 when the Nationalist leader Chiang Kai Shek, attacked the Communists and massacred most of them. The Comintern henceforth ordered the world's Communist parties not to co-operate with any other political party, even if it labelled itself Labour or Socialist. * This was to have one result of high consequence. In Germany, the sizeable Communist party attacked the Social Democrats almost as strongly as the Nazis, and this prevented the formation of a unified front against Hitler.

Meanwhile Russia, through the person of Maxim Litvinov, her Commissar for Foreign Affairs from 1930, continued to call for world peace and disarmament. The Soviet government was an early signatory of the Kellogg-Briand Pact renouncing war as a means of policy (BWE,

---

* Though Stalin continued to support Chiang Kai Shek until the end of the Second World War, because he mistakenly thought the Chinese Communists had little chance of securing power.

pp. 14–15), and arranged neutrality agreements with most of her European neighbours in the late 1920s and early 1930s.

(2) The Soviet Union and Nazi Germany, 1933–41

Russia joins the League   Hitler's assumption of power in Germany in 1933 was to prove a major turning-point in European history. Yet despite all he had written in *Mein Kampf* about turning eastern Europe and Russia into *Lebensraum* (living space) for the superior German race (BWE, pp. 36–7), and despite the conflict of ideology between fascism and communism, Stalin hoped that the co-operation begun at Rapallo would continue, even with Nazi Germany. But the potential danger was recognized when Hitler made a pact with Russia's western neighbour, Poland, in 1934. Czechoslovakia, Romania, and Bulgaria reacted by establishing diplomatic relations with Russia in 1934. The Russians themselves saw that isolation was potentially suicidal; and certainly so if Hitler joined Britain and France in an anti-communist alliance. So, in 1934, Russia joined the League of Nations, with a permanent seat on the Council (CORE, p. 50). In 1935 treaties with France and Czechoslovakia were turned into mutual defence arrangements, including a promise that Russia and France would aid Czechoslovakia if she were attacked — though Russia only agreed to do so provided France did so as well. The Soviet government would not act on its own.

'Popular Fronts' and Russian intervention in the Spanish Civil War   The folly of previous Comintern policy was recognized and in 1935 it was completely reversed. From now on, Communist parties were to join with any party, including even the Conservatives, in anti-fascist 'Popular Fronts'. A 'Popular Front' government, including the Communists, was formed in France in 1936 and the Communists gave their support to the Republican cause against General Franco in the Spanish Civil War. Stalin ordered them to adopt a very moderate policy which included respecting the rights of private property. He was loath to intervene in the war for fear of the hostile reaction a Communist victory might cause, especially in France, but he felt that the Soviet Union must back the Republicans in view of the support given by the Fascist powers, Germany and Italy, to Franco (CORE, p. 50). He hoped to keep the Germans occupied there for some time and divert their attention from eastern Europe. Yet only a limited amount of aid was sent; far less than German and Italian support for Franco. Moreover, part of Russian energies were spent on trying to crush anarchists and Trotskyists within the Spanish Republican forces.

The Japanese danger   By this time there was also danger to Russia in the Far East. Japan had seized Chinese Manchuria, an area of traditional Russian interest, and from late 1937 embarked on a conquest of China's eastern seaboard (AA, p. 22). The USA, also alarmed at Japanese aggression, finally recognized the Soviet government in 1933. In 1937 Russia signed a non-aggression pact with China, and before long her troops were involved in border incidents with the Japanese. The Japanese agreement with Germany in 1936, and with Italy in 1937, in the Anti-Comintern pact, plus Hitler's increasingly active policy in eastern Europe, made a war on two fronts a real possibility for the Soviet Union.

Stalin was alarmed at the possibility of war, especially since the Soviet

Union had no certain allies. The Western powers, Britain and France, were apparently doing all they could to appease Hitler (CORE, p. 51). In 1938 Hitler annexed Austria, and when he then turned to Czechoslovakia with demands for the Sudetenland, the British Prime Minister, Neville Chamberlain, hurried round Europe trying to find a peaceful solution to the problem. The French followed a similar policy; in particular they rejected the Russian proposal that they honour their recent agreement to defend the Czech state. Neither Russians nor Czechs were invited to the Munich Conference of September 1938, which gave Hitler what he wanted. In the following year, when Hitler broke this agreement with the final destruction of Czechoslovakia and then made demands for the Polish corridor and Danzig, Britain and France declared they would guarantee Poland. Stalin did not believe them. It appeared to him that the Western powers were attempting to avoid war at all costs. Many Western leaders were known to fear communist Russia more than Hitler's Germany, and the reliability of Russia as a military ally had been called into question by the recent purges of the armed forces (p. 58). Perhaps they were hoping for a Russio-German conflict in which Nazism and Communism would destroy each other. Stalin's doubts were only reinforced when Britain and France sent foreign office officials, rather than Cabinet ministers, to discuss concerted moves against Hitler in 1939.

A David Low cartoon on the Nazi-Soviet Pact of 1939

The Nazi-Soviet   Luckily for Stalin, Hitler did not yet wish to have a war with Russia,
Pact, 1939   especially as he could not be absolutely sure about British and French
intentions: Germany might face a war on two fronts. Stalin feared the outcome of war with Nazi Germany and had no scruples about doing all he
could to avoid it. So Litvinov, whose pro-Western attitude and Jewish birth
were a nuisance, was replaced by Molotov, and negotiations with Hitler's
Germany resulted in the Nazi-Soviet Pact of August 1939. Molotov and
Ribbentrop signed a 10-year Non-Aggression Pact for their respective
countries; in secret clauses they also agreed to a partition of Poland, Latvia,
and Estonia. Russia was to gain eastern Poland, Latvia, and Estonia, areas
lost during the period 1918–21. It was an agreement of mutual convenience.
Neither Hitler nor Stalin had any illusions about this. For Russia it bought
time, postponing the day when Hitler's ambitions in eastern Europe would
bring the inevitable conflict.

The partition of   German troops invaded Poland on 1 September 1939. Two days later
Poland,   Britain and France declared war, although they sent no troops to save the
September 1939 Polish state, which was quickly crushed. Stalin was alarmed at the speed of
the German victory, and on 17 September Russian troops entered eastern
Poland and quickly overran it. (Two days earlier Russia had terminated
hostilities with Japan in the Far East.)

The Russo-   With Europe at war Stalin set about strengthening Russia's position in the
Finnish war   Baltic. New agreements with Hitler gave Lithuania to Russia, and in the
(1939-40)   following two years the Baltic states became part of the USSR. Russia began
to supply Germany with raw materials for her war effort, especially grain,
metals, and petrol. (She was still honouring these agreements when German
troops turned on Russia in 1941). Negotiations were also opened with
Finland to alter Russia's border near Leningrad, which was extremely
vulnerable. The Finns refused to accept the Russian proposals, so Stalin
ordered Russian troops to attack in November 1939. The following month
the USSR was expelled from the League of Nations. The outcome of the war
was never in doubt; but the contrast between Hitler's lightning successes
and the difficulties experienced by the Russian forces were plain for all to
see. Finnish resistance and the problems of fighting in the snow, among the
swamps, lakes, and forests of Finland, prolonged the war until February
1940, when the Finnish effort collapsed. Russia then insisted on the border
adjustment she had previously demanded.

(3) The War comes to Russia — 1941

Following the war with Finland Stalin forced the Romanians to return to
Russia the area of Bessarabia that they had gained in 1918. He had imagined
Hitler would leave the Balkan area to Russia, and was alarmed when
German troops entered Romania in October 1940, despite Russian
objections. Hitler now ordered his military command to prepare specific
plans for an invasion of Russia in 1941. At four o'clock in the morning of 22
The German   June 1941 a huge German army of at least three million men launched a
invasion   three-pronged attack on Soviet Russia as laid down in the plan 'Operation
Barbarossa' (CORE, p. 61). Soviet intelligence had indicated that German
troop movements and reconnaissance flights pointed to war in the very near

future, and Winston Churchill had even told Stalin of the exact date. Stalin refused to believe that Hitler was about to break his agreement and was in fact away on the Black Sea coast when the invasion started. The armed forces were given so short a warning that they were unable to put up effective resistance. The army was ill-prepared anyway. Some attempt had been made to train new recruits and to improve the efficiency of the fighting units since the Finnish war, and some new weapons such as the T-34 tank were under production. There were, however, not enough of them, and much of the rest of Soviet weaponry was out of date. The Soviet armies reeled, while Stalin himself seemed to be in a state of total shock for several days.

German troops invading Russia, 1941

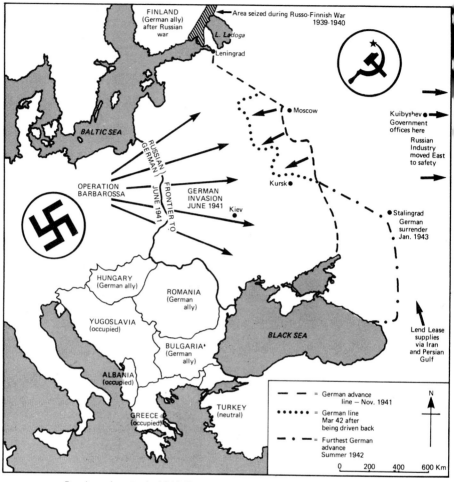

Russia under attack, 1941–3

Western Russia overrun

The speed of the German advance gave no time for preparing adequate defences in the western areas. Some 2000 Russian planes were destroyed in the first two days of fighting and mastery of the air enabled the Germans to slaughter or capture many thousands of Russian soldiers. The Nazi armies moved swiftly through the land the Soviet Union had taken from Poland. By August Leningrad was threatened, and in September Kiev fell, the Germans capturing some half a million Russians in the process. In Moscow a five-man State Committee for Defence was organized, with Stalin assuming overall command of operations, though the actual direction of the army was left to Marshal Zhukov. Stalin made a first broadcast to the nation on 3 July. He called the German attack treacherous and at the same time defended his original agreement as having bought Russia nearly two years of peace in which to prepare for the expected attack. He rallied the Russians to defend their country, and, where retreat was necessary, to adopt a policy of 'scorched earth', destroying anything of use that had to be left behind. In

'Scorched earth' policy

this way the advancing German forces would not be able to live off the land they conquered. Much of Russian industry and good farming land was directly in the path of the enemy advance. Where possible, valuable equipment and materials were moved east; whole factories were dismantled in a mammoth operation and transported into central and eastern Russia where they were soon reconstructed and put back into operation. Between July and November 1941 some 1523 industrial enterprises were moved (1360 of them large-scale) and 10 million people evacuated. But industrial production inevitably slumped to half that of the previous year, just when full output was vital.

Moscow threatened Moscow itself came under threat in October 1941 and industries and all non-essential personnel were ordered to leave. Government departments were evacuated to Kuibyshev on the Volga. On 2 October Hitler issued his orders: 'Today is the beginning of the last great decisive battle of this year.' A feeling that Moscow was about to surrender caused panic; but this was lessened by the knowledge that Stalin remained in the Kremlin and that the defences of the city were being organized. On the anniversary of the 1917 revolution Stalin again rallied his people, referring to the Germans' racial arrogance:

> These people with the morality of animals . . . want a war of extermination against the peoples of the Soviet Union. Very well then! If they want a war of extermination, they shall have it!

During the war there was a great upsurge of national feeling which was encouraged by the government. The Russians called the war 'the Great Patriotic War'. Peace was made with the previously persecuted Church, for religious fervour could be used to encourage greater efforts against Hitlerism. At the centre was Stalin himself, the great hero and mastermind of the Russian war effort. Symbolic of this was the new national anthem introduced in 1944 to replace the revolutionary 'Internationale'. It included the words:

> Unbreakable union of free born republics,
> Great Russia has welded forever to stand,

and continued:

> Stalin raised us and inspired us
> To be true to the people, to work
> To perform heroic deeds.

The German forces halted — winter 1941 In places the German forces got to the very outskirts of Moscow. But the advance had slowed down. The troops were weary, supply-lines had become extended because of the speed of the advance, and the Russian winter was setting in. The temperature soon dropped to 40 degrees below zero, petrol froze in the engines, and the soldiers, under-equipped for the climate, suffered severe frost-bite. The Russians launched their first counter-attacks and were able to drive the Germans back. The new T-34 tanks played a decisive role. In some places the Russians advanced up to 320 kilometres and Moscow was for the time being saved, though lack of war materials meant that the advances could not be fully exploited.

Leningrad under   Leningrad, meanwhile, was also under siege. The Germans had begun
siege   their bombardment of the city in September 1941 and had virtually isolated
it from the rest of the country. Only one line of communication across the ice
of Lake Ladoga was maintained. The evacuation of the very old and very
young had not been organized in time and food and fuel supplies soon
dropped below survival level. Only in February 1942 did conditions
improve somewhat, and by then the death toll was well above a quarter of a
million.

The occupied   As the Germans advanced they were welcomed in some areas as liberators
areas   from communism. People hoped for an end to the collectives and for the
possibility of establishing their own independent national states under
German supervision. As one collective farmer wrote:

> At first the Germans were friendly; they accepted the food they were offered,
> clicked their cameras and roared 'Stalin kaput'. But the 'liberation' did not last
> long. In the winter of 1942 the Germans ordered the restoration of the kolkhozes.
> . . . Regulations became stricter than ever.

Any initial goodwill soon disappeared as the cruel behaviour of the German
troops and the German plans for Russia were revealed. To the Germans
western Russia was 'living space' — a vast storehouse of food and raw
materials for Germany. The Russians were lesser beings, *Untermenschen*,
whose sole use was as a ready supply of labour. Nearly three million young
Forced labour   Russians were sent to Germany to work in war industries. Known
Communists were shot or transported to concentration camps further west.
The same fate awaited the Jews, whose extermination was now
Extermination   ordered. Mass graves were later found, often of women and children shot in
of the Jews   the back. At Babi Yar, near Kiev, the remains of 100 000 Jews were later
uncovered. Prisoners of war were herded into large camps without adequate
POWs   food, medical attention or protection against the severe winters. Epidemics
were rampant and the death rate enormous. When the Soviet armies re-
occupied western Russia in 1943–4 millions of people had simply
disappeared without trace. Huge city populations had been reduced by half.

Some Russians chose to fight against the Communist government of their
country and an 'Army of Liberation' was established in 1942. Hitler made
little use of this, for it did not fit in with his racial ideas to have Russians
fighting as equals alongside the 'master race'. At the other extreme, partisan
resistance groups sprang up to sabotage the German occupation and to hold
The resistance   down huge numbers of troops which could then not be sent to the
battlefront. By 1943 there were over half a million active armed partisans.
The German reaction was savage: whole villages were destroyed and their
inhabitants disappeared or were shot. This only bred further resistance.

(4) The Battle for Stalingrad and the Russian Triumph, 1942–45

German advance   The summer of 1942 saw a new German offensive launched for the capture
in southern   of the industrial complex of the Donbas region and the Caucasus oil fields.
Russia, 1942   The Russians suffered further disastrous losses and by September the
Germans were ready to launch their attack on the sprawling industrial town
of Stalingrad (CORE, p. 63). It was here that the Russians were ordered to

retreat no further. Incessant bombardment from September to November reduced most of the city to rubble, but the Germans failed to break through. In mid-November the Russians launched a massive counter-attack and encircled the German Sixth Army. Von Paulus, its commander, wished to make terms as winter set in, but Hitler refused to countenance such a move, even though the troops were short of all essential supplies. On the last day of January 1943 the German army finally gave in. Of the 330 000 German soldiers sent to Stalingrad there were only 93 000 left alive to surrender.

German surrender

The Russians had been making gigantic efforts on the production front to compensate for their lost lands and industrial potential. By the time of the battle for Stalingrad the Soviet Union was producing more tanks and planes than Germany and had increased her arms output four-fold since 1941. The concentration on military equipment was almost total. Shoes and clothing were in very short supply, and food had to be rationed, as much of the best agricultural land was under German occupation. Some of the shortfall was made up by supplies from Russia's allies, especially from the USA under the Lend-Lease arrangement.

The Battle of Stalingrad was a turning point. Early in 1943, the Red Armies made substantial advances. These took the pressure off both Moscow and Leningrad. Despite some successful German counter-attacks the Russian momentum was maintained. Hitler's armies made an enormous effort to reverse this tide in the summer of 1943. Some 3000 tanks and 2000 aircraft were sent to aid them at Kursk, but their efforts failed. From that point on the German armies were in retreat and a German defeat was inevitable. By the end of the year two-thirds of the areas previously lost by the USSR had been regained in fierce fighting, and the Red armies began to move into the neighbouring states. Russian troops entered Romania in March 1944 and took the capital, Bucharest, in August. A new government was set up and Romania then joined the war against the Germans. In September Bulgaria did likewise, while the Finns agreed to an armistice; in October the Baltic States were taken; in the same month Yugoslav Partisans and Russian troops entered Belgrade. In Poland the Russians reached the outskirts of Warsaw by July. The inhabitants of the capital staged an uprising against the Germans to coincide with the hoped-for Russian help. However, the Russians hung back; the rising was crushed by the Germans and the city was destroyed. Only in January 1945 did Russian troops move. The Russians were much criticized for their delay, and the anti-communist nature of the leaders of the rising is usually assumed to be the reason for the inaction. Stalin claimed simply that the rising was premature.

The battle for Kursk

Russian troops enter eastern Europe

As the war drew to a close in the early months of 1945 Russian troops became the masters of eastern and central Europe, occupying Warsaw, Budapest and Vienna — capitals of Poland, Hungary and Austria respectively — as they moved on Germany. Finally in May 1945 Russian troops seized Berlin, and Hitler committed suicide as they approached. On 8 May the Germans surrendered; on the following day Russian troops entered the Czech capital, Prague. The war in Europe was over.

Berlin falls — victory in Europe

Victorious Russians in Berlin, 1945

(5) Wartime Diplomacy

Stalin's wartime diplomacy had three main aims. The first was to obtain as much Allied support as possible in the fight against Nazi Germany; the second, to get Russia's recent gains — the Baltic States, Eastern Poland, parts of Finland and Bessarabia — recognized by his allies; and the third, to prepare the way for Russian domination of the lands to the west of her border at the end of the conflict.

With the German invasion of June 1941 previous Anglo-Russian hostility was quickly submerged in the face of mutual danger. Winston Churchill announced:

> The Russian danger is our danger . . . the cause of any Russian fighting for his hearth and home is the cause of free men and free people in every quarter of the globe.

The USA, not yet in the war, extended the Lend-Lease arrangements to Russia and supplied $145 million worth of goods in the first three months.

British and Russian troops occupied areas of Iran to secure a supply route through the Persian Gulf since shipping in the North Atlantic was so much at risk. Stalin welcomed this aid, but also called for a landing in western Europe to take the pressure off the Russians (CORE, p. 66). He failed to appreciate why this could not be done straight away, and his calls became more insistent during 1942 and 1943. The savagery and the enormous casualties suffered in Russia make it easy to understand the importance he attached to a second front, an Allied landing in western Europe. However, it was not to take place until June 1944.

Relations between the Allies remained cordial and as a gesture of friendship Stalin dissolved the Comintern in 1943. The three wartime leaders (Stalin, Churchill, and the American President, Franklin Roosevelt) met together for the first time at Teheran in November 1943. The question of British and American landings on the continent was thoroughly aired and Churchill proposed that one such landing should be made in the Balkans. Stalin was aware that this could prevent complete Russian domination of the area after the war and he was totally opposed to Churchill's plans. He got his way because Roosevelt was against such a landing on military grounds. Britain and the United States were prepared to recognize Russia's gains between 1939 and 1941 and the new Polish frontier was agreed as the Curzon line. This was the border laid down at Versailles in 1919 and was far more generous to Russia than her boundary before hostilities broke out in 1939. In 1944 Churchill also agreed to Romania, Hungary, and Bulgaria coming within Russia's sphere of influence after the war. It was decided that Greece was to be in Britain's sphere and Yugoslavia was to be 50:50.

As the war in Europe drew to a close the 'Big Three' met again at Yalta in the Crimea in February 1945 (CORE, p. 74). They agreed that after Germany's unconditional surrender she should be demilitarized, denazified, and divided into zones of occupation for the Allies. Germany would also have to pay reparations for war damage. The United Nations Organization was to be established and each great power was to have the right of veto on resolutions. This point was particularly insisted upon by Stalin. Informally Stalin agreed at Yalta that Russia would enter the war against Japan two to three months after the close of the European war and, in return, would regain lands lost to Japan in 1905. The question of Poland was less easy to settle. Churchill and Roosevelt hoped that the country could be saved from complete domination by the Russians, who had recently installed the Communist, and Moscow-based, Lublin government (so called from the town which was its original headquarters). They wanted members of the Polish government in exile in London to be included and Stalin at this stage agreed and also promised 'free and unfettered elections'.

Calls for 'second front'

The Teheran Conference, 1943

The Yalta Conference, 1945

Part II
Eastern Europe between the Wars

7

Eastern Europe 1918–39

(1) The Legacy of the First World War

Before the First World War central and eastern Europe were dominated by the great empires of Germany, Russia and Austria-Hungary. These empires contained peoples of many different nationalities who wanted more control over their own affairs. They disliked in particular the rule of a foreign royal family, foreign officials, and perhaps domination by an alien aristocracy as well. The disintegration of the European empires and their defeat during the war gave their subject peoples the chance to establish their own independent states. They were encouraged in this by the Western powers who saw small, independent and democratic states as their natural future allies. Woodrow Wilson in his 14 Points spoke of national self-determination, of different peoples deciding their own futures. After the Bolshevik revolution in Russia the peace-makers also saw these new states as a potential barrier against the 'new disease from the East', communism. The peace treaties of 1919–20 recognized the break-up of the old empires, and the new independent states of Austria,* Hungary, Poland, Czechoslovakia, Estonia, Latvia and Lithuania, emerged. They joined the Balkan states of Bulgaria, Romania, Albania and Serbia (now joined with the Slav lands of the Habsburg Empire to form Yugoslavia), which had won their independence from the crumbling Ottoman or Turkish Empire during the 19th and early 20th centuries; a patchwork of states was thus created which stretched from the Baltic to the Black and Mediterranean Seas.

Democracy fails to develop   The Western powers had high hopes for the development of democracy in these new 'succession' states (the name given to those into which the Habsburg Empire was broken up), but the hopes proved to be short-lived.

* For the history of Austria since 1918, see BWE, pp. 7, 67, 74.

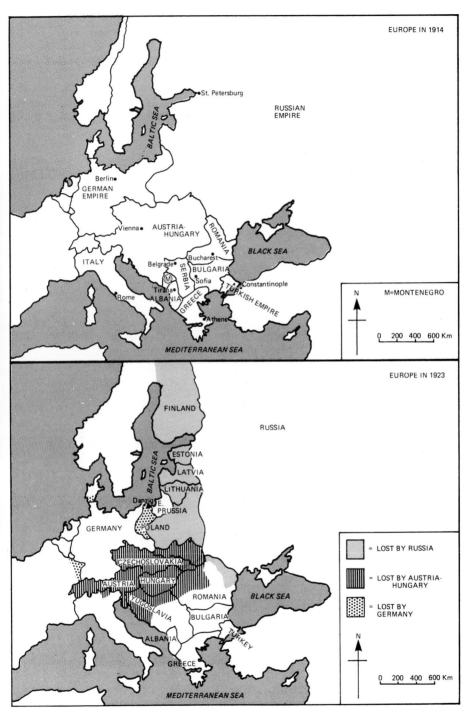

A comparison of Eastern Europe before and after the First World War

Eastern Europe between the wars; the clearly drawn frontiers conceal the many disputes over land that remained

Many never really adopted democratic procedures; others did so but found them unworkable, and they were soon overthrown by leaders and parties who saw them as having no value in their situation. This is not altogether surprising, for democratic regimes require certain conditions in which to grow and these were missing in practically all these countries. First there was little tradition of self-rule by individual countries, let alone by the people within them. The peasants who made up the majority of the population had little education or political knowledge, but plenty of experience at accepting orders from landlords and far-off royal courts. Very often the ruling classes had little desire to alter the status quo. Secondly, the new

Economic
problems

states had many economic problems, the major one being poverty. They were all, with the exception of Czechoslovakia, predominantly agricultural; in most, farming methods were primitive and the population too large for the land available. They had little industry and little money with which to build it up. There was equally little money available for modernizing farming methods. The new frontiers which split up the empires often did not make economic sense. For example, Slovakia found itself cut off from its old markets in Hungary; the 'succession' states from the Austrian Empire inherited a communications network suited to the old boundaries rather than their own national needs. Many of the countries soon put up tariff barriers and charged high customs duties on imported goods, as a means of protecting their own industry and agriculture. This reduced trade and made the economic situation more difficult.

Farming in Eastern Europe

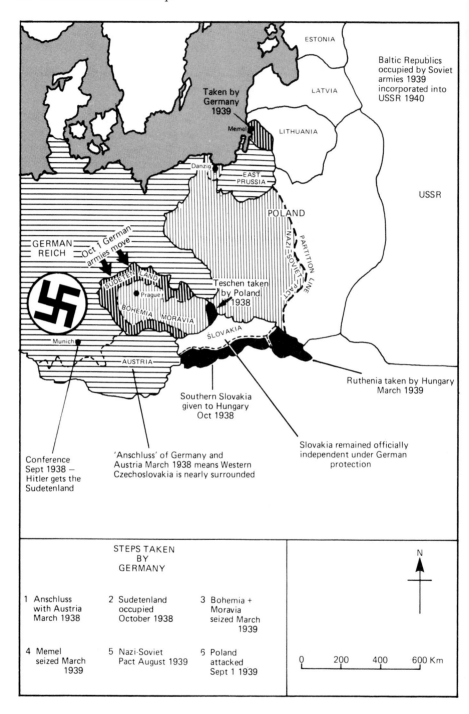

The destruction of Eastern European independence, 1938–9

The 1920s proved problematic with short periods of prosperity; the 1930s with the world recession were devastating. The economic dislocation and resulting hardship gave rise to violent political disagreements and extremist political parties, especially right-wing Fascist parties. The give-and-take of democratic states, where political leaders were prepared to rely on winning power through the ballot box and to put up with long periods in opposition, proved to be missing. The Western powers' belief that they could export Western-style democracy to areas less developed both politically and economically than their own was found to be unrealistic. Political instability gave way to authoritarian government. The international situation and the threat to the security of the small states caused by the activities of Mussolini and Hitler reinforced this trend.

Quarrels over land   The new countries had grown out of the collapse of German and Russian power. It was questionable whether their independence would survive its revival. Unfortunately, the patchwork of states had quarrels among themselves which resulted from their frontiers. The peace-makers had done what they could to draw lines around different national groups, but this was not possible where different nationalities were very mixed up. They had also had to take account of economic and defence needs. Countries needed good farming land and, where possible, industry to survive.

The problem of minorities   Moreover, most of the new states had substantial national minorities within their borders. The new Poland was about 70% Polish but had large German, Ukrainian, and Jewish minorities. Czechoslovakia was 65% Czech and Slovak but had considerable numbers of Germans and Hungarians. The minorities often resented their position especially when the economic situation deteriorated. In the 1930s their grievances were used by other countries to stir up trouble. The most obvious example was the use that Hitler made of the German minorities in Poland and Czechoslovakia to upset the international scene for the benefit of Nazi Germany. Yet from the start several of the new states were 'revisionist' — that is, they wanted to revise the new frontiers as laid down in the post-war treaties to get lands they believed should have been theirs. Hungary was the prime example, for the old Hungarian lands within the Habsburg Empire had been reduced to one third of their former size by the Treaty of Trianon. Such squabbles weakened the resolve of the small states to stand together and deprived the area of any strength it could have gained from unity. Most of the countries fell under Nazi rule within 20 years of their establishment. They were not to emerge again as independent peoples, for the Nazi domination was replaced after the Second World War by that of the Soviet Union.

(2) The Baltic Republics

The Baltic Republics of Latvia, Lithuania and Estonia were removed from Russia by the Treaty of Brest-Litovsk and assured of their independence by the Treaty of Versailles. Each state set up a democratic system of government and introduced land reforms to help the peasants. Economic difficulties and political instability, with frequent changes of government, led to the establishment of military dictatorships. The first to go under was Lithuania in 1926; the other two democracies survived until the depression years.

Their internal difficulties were added to by outside enemies. Poland seized Vilna from Lithuania in 1920, and Nazi Germany took Memel from the same state in 1939. They were all occupied by Soviet troops after 1939 and incorporated into the USSR, where they have since remained.

(3) Poland

Poland had existed as a separate state until the late 18th century when it had been partitioned by its three great neighbours, Prussia, Russia and Austria. By 1918 the Western Allies were committed to its revival: Wilson's 13th Point promised this, together with an outlet to the sea. This was duly given in the 'Polish corridor' and the use of the port of Danzig. The industrial area of Upper Silesia was added after a plebiscite in 1920. Poland's eastern border was established on what was known as the Curzon Line. Of all the new states Poland was the one that most depended on a weak Germany and a weak Russia for existence. Her very creation angered the Germans who looked down on the Poles. They resented the loss of the German port of Danzig and the fact that the 'Polish corridor' cut off East Prussia from the rest of Germany. The enmity of Soviet Russia resulted from the Russo-Polish war of 1920–1 when the Polish forces took the opportunity of the Russian Civil War to detach a further slice of land from the western reaches of that country. She made a third enemy in 1920 by seizing the town of Vilna from Lithuania.

German and Soviet enmity

The most notable Polish statesman of the post-war years was Josef Pilsudski, the fiery leader of the national wing of the Polish Socialists. He became President of the new republic and it was his adventurous policy that led to the attack on Russia and the seizure of Vilna. He was most fiercely opposed by the National Democrats, led by Roman Dmowski, who wanted friendly relations with Russia, to combat the threat of a revived Germany. Dmowski's party dominated the National Assembly, the Polish Parliament, in its early years. When they drew up the new constitution under which Poland was to be governed they limited the authority of the President, to cut Pilsudski's power, and he resigned in protest. Most power was given to the lower house of Parliament, the Sjem. The constitution was modelled on the French one and included proportional representation. This soon led to the formation of a large number of political parties. There were 92 by 1925, and 32 of them were represented in the Sjem. The formation of strong governments was almost impossible and there were 14 different ones between 1918 and 1926. Political instability frequently gave way to violence. In 1922, for example, Pilsudski's successor as President, Narutowicz, was assassinated after only two days in office.

Political instability

The economy was equally unstable. Poland had suffered extensive wartime devastation, and the economies and communications of areas formerly in three different empires had to be integrated. The country was 75% agricultural and poor and the early 1920s witnessed the Polish mark declining in value nearly as rapidly as the German currency. In 1918 one American dollar bought 9·8 Polish marks; in 1923 2·3 million Polish marks. There were strikes and violence in the industrial areas. A new currency, the zloty, was introduced in 1924, but there were further economic problems

Economic problems

and inflation in 1925.

In May 1926, tired of the unstable political and economic situation, Pilsudski and his followers marched on Warsaw and seized power. Pilsudski became virtual dictator of the country until his death in 1935. Though not a harsh dictatorship, the government did manipulate the elections to make sure its own 'Non-Party' bloc won. Pilsudski himself only held the office of Prime Minister twice, but he remained the power behind the scenes. He took his advice from a selection of very conservative colonels. Although he had formerly called himself a socialist, Pilsudski failed to carry out social reforms, and when Poland was severely hit by the world depression and collapse of agricultural prices his government had no answer. This led to the rise of very radical Nationalist parties who admired their Fascist German neighbours. Poland's three million Jews, many of whom had been active in business affairs, became the scapegoats for the economic ills. They were ousted from government monopolies in trade and from the civil service, and their businesses were boycotted.

Marshal Pilsudski

The threat to Poland's existence   No totally dominant leader emerged after Pilsudski's death in 1935. The Poles became increasingly concerned with the international situation, but for a long time the Foreign Minister, Josef Beck, did not seem to take the threat from Nazi Germany seriously. A non-aggression pact was signed with Hitler in 1934, and the government hoped for some kind of bargain over Danzig and the Polish corridor. They joined in Hitler's carve-up of the Czech state in 1938, and received Teschen, which they had demanded since 1920. When their own turn came to face German demands in 1939 they lessened their chances of survival by refusing any agreement which might allow Russian troops on their soil. In fact the British, French and Russian talks for possible co-operation against Nazi Germany finally broke down on that very point. The Poles probably hoped they could play off Russia and Germany against each other and thus ensure their own survival. But the Nazi-Soviet Pact of August 1939 and subsequent German and Soviet invasions obliterated their state exactly 20 years after its revival (CORE pp. 50, 52, 54).

(4) Hungary

Hungary had had considerable status within the Habsburg Empire, which had officially been known as Austria-Hungary since 1867. Independence as a separate country followed the collapse of the Habsburg Empire in 1918. The first Prime Minister after the war was the moderate Count Michael Karolyi who wished to set up a democratic regime, break up the large landed estates, and distribute the land among the peasants. He handed over his own lands as a first step. When he realized that the Allies were going to make a harsh peace with Hungary as a defeated nation, he resigned and the more radical Social Democrats took over. They allied with the Communists who

Bela Kun's Soviet Republic overthrown   established a Soviet republic under the leadership of a Jewish revolutionary Bela Kun. This was short-lived and brought down by a combination of Romanian and Hungarian troops under the former commander of the Habsburg navy, Admiral Horthy. His forces unleashed a 'white terror' in

Admiral Horthy   which potential left-wingers, notably workers and peasants, and Jews (many of whom had supported Kun) were massacred. An election was held for a new government during the terror and Horthy was then established as Regent of the country. This was supposedly on behalf of the Habsburgs but they were not allowed to return and he remained head of state for life with considerable powers. Horthy was a very conservative landowner and the estates already seized were handed back to their previous owners, with the exception of Karolyi's. Large-scale businesses were given a free hand.

The Treaty of Trianon   The regime was forced to accept the Treaty of Trianon in June 1920 which deprived traditional Hungary of two-thirds of its lands and left three million Magyars (the name of the Hungarian people) beyond its borders. There were 1·7 million in Transylvania, which went to Romania; a further million in Slovakia and Ruthenia, which went to Czechoslovakia; and a further 500 000 in Yugoslavia. Hungary became a revisionist power and very nationalistic in her outlook. She did not therefore get on well with her three neighbours who had Magyar minorities, and they in fact combined against her by forming the 'Little Entente' in 1921. Hungary's foreign policy naturally drew her towards the other main revisionist powers, Italy and Germany.

Hungary had one of the most right-wing authoritarian regimes in the inter-war years. The right to vote was severely restricted to certain property-owners, and voting in the countryside was open, which allowed the government and aristocracy to intimidate the voters. Anyone vaguely radical was suspected of being a Communist and badly treated. Workers were forbidden to organize trade unions, liberals and Jews were kept from teaching posts. Jews, in particular, were discriminated against. They were turned out of university posts and the number of Jewish students was severely limited; they could not enter government employment or buy land for farming. Many semi-military organizations were established, the most important being the fanatically Nationalist and anti-semitic Hungarian Association for National Defence. This was led by an ex-army officer of German origin, Julius Gömbös. In 1920 Hungary supported the Nationalist Kapp putsch in Germany and even tried to wreck liberal regimes she did not like by flooding their countries with forged banknotes. A plot of this nature was uncovered in Belgium in 1926.

The Prime Minister until 1931 was Count Stephen Bethlen, who presided over a relatively stable era. The currency was set in order and inflation was eased by a foreign loan of 250 million crowns, which was given on condition that Hungary reaffirm her willingness to abide by the Treaty of Trianon. Industrial production more than doubled in 10 years and even agriculture prospered. But the Wall Street crash and resulting depression ruined the country. The slump in world agricultural prices reduced the peasants to subsistence farming and the business world was shaken by the collapse of the main Austrian bank, the 'Kreditanstalt', in 1931, which brought down with it the central European banking system.

Bethlen resigned in 1931 and within a year Julius Gömbös had become Premier. He watched possible opposition and the press closely and moved his supporters into the civil service and army. He formed his own party, the 'Movement for National Unity' and was planning to bring in a full fascist dictatorship when he died in 1936. Attracted by the fascist regimes and the revival of Germany, Gömbös had formed close ties with Italy and Germany. The latter came to dominate Hungary's foreign trade. Between 1934 and 1937 Hungary's imports from Germany (mainly manufactured goods) doubled, and her own farm exports trebled. Gömbös' successors were equally right-wing and they continued the move into Hitler's camp. They took on more of the trappings of the Nazi regime, including anti-Jewish laws. Hungary was rewarded by gaining southern Slovakia from Czechoslovakia in November 1938; she received Ruthenia the next year. By this time she was also a member of the anti-Comintern pact alongside Germany, Italy and Japan.

(5) Romania

Pre-First World War Romania was very typical of eighteenth- and nineteenth-century Europe. She was 80% agricultural, her serfs had only been freed in 1864 and the country continued to be dominated by the king and rich landlords. Trade, looked down upon by the aristocracy, was mainly in the hands of Greeks and Jews and their wealth helped to make them unpopular. The only industry of any size was the oil industry, centred on the wells at Ploesti. Because Romania fought on the Allied side from 1916, the country was rewarded with substantial territorial gains, which nearly doubled her size, at the end of the war. Transylvania was acquired from Hungary and Bessarabia from Russia. These gains brought large minorities and foreign enemies who wanted their lands back.

King Ferdinand and his nobles feared the spread of Bolshevism and brought in land reform to lessen its appeal to the peasantry. About four million hectares from the large estates were distributed among the peasants. However, this failed to bring prosperity because the new owners lacked both the expertise and the money to invest in improvements and machinery. They were also heavily taxed by a government, which initially did not wish to have foreign money flowing into its industry, and which then relied on taxes to finance industrial development.

Crown Prince Carol of Romania, King Ferdinand of Romania and King Alexander of Yugoslavia

The monarchy   Although universal male suffrage was introduced, the king still retained control of the country. Even elections could be manipulated through the Civil Service and army. Political life was corrupt and many politicians did very well for themselves, especially those in the Liberal Party, on whom the king relied. Ferdinand forced his son Carol into exile on account of his scandalous private life and half-Jewish mistress, and on Ferdinand's death in 1927, there were two years of relatively democratic rule, until Carol returned in 1930, bringing his mistress, Madame Lupescu, with him. He ruled in an increasingly dictatorial way, finally bringing in a new constitution in 1938 which abolished the political party system and enormously increased the king's power over Parliament. The 1930s witnessed in Romania, as elsewhere, the growth of radical right-wing parties. The major one was 'the Iron Guard' which called for radical land reform and anti-Jewish laws. Carol was not above encouraging violent attacks on Jews but did not wish to share power with the increasingly powerful Iron Guard. He arranged for their main leaders to be arrested, and then 'shot while trying to escape' in 1938.

Links with Nazi Germany

The international scene in the late 1930s brought rapid changes to eastern Europe. Carol attempted to stay neutral, but increasingly drifted into the German camp. In 1939 an important economic treaty was signed allowing joint German-Romanian development of Romania's resources. Hitler wanted Romania's oil. However, he also ordered Romania to give up lands to Russia, Bulgaria, and Hungary to suit his own international schemes. These losses made Carol so unpopular that he was forced to abdicate in favour of his son Michael. The monarchy was only allowed to continue on the understanding that full powers were given to a military regime with 'Iron Guard' participation, which was established under General Ion Antonescu. This then sought full German protection. Romania joined the attack on the USSR in June 1941.

(6) Bulgaria

Bulgaria had fought alongside the Central Powers in the First World War and by the Treaty of Neuilly was forced to accept land losses to Yugoslavia and, more importantly, to Greece, which deprived her of an outlet on the Aegean Sea.

Political instability

Bulgaria was a country of peasants and small landowners in which the monarch, King Boris, retained considerable authority. In the years immediately after the war power lay with the veteran peasant leader, Alexander Stamboliiski, who introduced a radical land reform to break up the remaining large estates. His ideas for ending the monarchy brought about his downfall and murder in 1923. An ill-considered Communist uprising in the same year was savagely put down. Violence became commonplace. In 1925 the Communists attempted to blow up the king in Sofia Cathedral but failed; their party was banned and an anti-left-wing witch hunt followed. The country was increasingly dominated by IMRO, the Internal Macedonian Revolutionary Organization, a terrorist movement which wanted to win back Macedonian lands in Greece and Yugoslavia. One section of IMRO was supported by the king, and another by Moscow, and Mussolini gave financial support in return for the trouble the organization could cause in Yugoslavia. In 1934 King Boris supported a military take-over in which IMRO was destroyed and order restored, but he then

Dictatorship

quarrelled with the army leaders, and from 1935 gradually established a personal dictatorship.

Bulgaria tried to stay neutral in the international quarrels of the late 1930s and Boris even established friendlier relations with the traditional enemy, Yugoslavia.

(7) Yugoslavia

The new state of Yugoslavia, the country of the South Slavs, was composed of pre-war independent Serbia, with lands from the Austro-Hungarian Empire. These included areas along the Dalmatian coast promised to Italy by the secret Treaty of London in 1915, and it was not until 1924 that the frontier was finally settled with Mussolini's Italy taking the disputed port of Fiume. Yugoslavia's official title was the kingdom of the Serbs, Croats, and

National and Slovenes, a name which recognized the three major nationalities in the nine
religious which made up the new country. National differences were underlined by
differences the variety of languages and alphabets used and the different religions

The map of present-day Yugoslavia with its six republics and two autonomous regions, indicates its many different peoples (see pp. 135–8)

practised. Quarrels soon broke out over how much control each area was to have over its own affairs, with the Croat Peasant Party delegates walking out of the talks on the new constitution. The rights of the different nationalities were lost in the highly centralized government which was imposed, and the Serbs and their king came to dominate the state. Political life became unstable. The fairly popular Communist Party was banned after a Communist assassinated the Minister of the Interior in 1921; the Croat Peasant Party veered from co-operation with the Serbs to total opposition. In 1928 a radical member of Parliament from Montenegro shot dead three Croat deputies including their leader, Radic. The violence and corruption of political life in no way benefited the country which remained 80% agricultural and poor. A mild measure of land distribution had hardly affected the basic poverty, as it simply led to a large number of small uneconomic farms. As elsewhere there were too many people for the land available, especially in view of the lack of industry.

Dictatorship   In January 1929 King Alexander, tired of the violence, political quarrelling and lack of national unity, established a dictatorship. As a sign of his intentions he changed the name of the country simply to Yugoslavia and he then proceeded to ban all political parties based on a region or religion. A new constitution in 1931 made government ministers responsible to the king rather than Parliament, and government powers were increased by replacing the secret ballot at election times with open voting. The first election, in 1931, which took place in the years of the depression, was characterized by government terror and the arrest of opposition leaders. In 1932 King Alexander starvation in the countryside and more arrests led to serious riots and in 1934 assassinated Alexander was assassinated in Marseilles while on an official visit to France. His assassin was a Macedonian terrorist who had the secret support of both the Italian and Hungarian governments.

A regency was established for Alexander's young son, Peter, and the Regent, Paul, attemped to ease the political situation. He released many of the political prisoners and allowed opposition parties to stand in the 1935 election. As the international situation became more serious Paul saw the urgency of maintaining national unity and he came to an agreement with the Croat Peasant Party in 1939. A new constitution gave considerable power to the different areas of the country, but this had little chance to work before the onset of war.

Invasion and   Yugoslavia attempted to remain neutral when war broke out in September partition 1939. This proved impossible, for when Mussolini's invasion of Greece ran into trouble and Hitler was planning to send help he forced the Yugoslavs to join the Anti-Comintern Pact in March 1941. The Serbs, who were traditionally pro-Russian, could not tolerate this and the Regent was overthrown. Hitler's troops then smashed Yugoslavia in April 1941 and the country was broken up. Germany, Italy, Hungary, and Bulgaria all gained areas and Croatia was declared independent under Italian and later German protection.

(8) Albania

A separate state of Albania had been created on Austrian insistence in 1912 to deprive Serbia of an outlet to the sea. It remained in existence after the war with both Italy and Yugoslavia trying to dominate it. Tribal leader Ahmed Zog seized power and made himself King Zog in 1928. He became very dependent on Mussolini for economic and military aid, and the Italians finally occupied the country in 1939 (CORE, p. 46).

(9) Czechoslovakia

Czechoslovakia was born out of the collapse of Austria-Hungary in 1918. The Czechs in the provinces of Bohemia and Moravia had hoped that the war would bring them a greater measure of self-rule. They realized that this could only occur if Germany and Austria-Hungary were defeated. Many of the Czechs therefore went into exile and fought alongside the Allies. The most active Czech leader abroad was Thomas Masaryk, the leader of the Czech Popular Party and ex-professor of philosophy at Prague University. A moderate man, who commanded great respect both at home and abroad, he worked hard to get the Allies to accept the idea of a Czechoslovak state. A Czech National Committee assumed full control in Prague on 28 October 1918. Two days later the leaders of the province of Slovakia, who had had few links with the Czechs previously, but had been dominated by the Hungarian landlords, voted to join the new state to form Czechoslovakia. Initially, there was some question as to what would happen to the 3½ million Germans on the border areas of Bohemia and Moravia. Most of them either wished to remain with the German-speaking Austrians or wanted to form a central European German state with Germany and Austria. The Czech leaders, however, wished to preserve Bohemia and Moravia intact and their troops occupied the border areas. The peace-makers recognized this situation and also hived off Ruthenia from Hungary and gave it to the new state. The Hungarians very much resented their losses, especially that of Slovakia. They attempted to disrupt the new state by encouraging Slovak independence movements which they, as rulers, had formerly tried to crush.

Czechoslovakia was very much an exception in the new eastern European scene, in that it had a well-balanced economy with considerable industrial development. In fact the new state contained two-thirds of the previous Austro-Hungarian Empire's industry, though only one quarter of its population. The industries she inherited included coal-mining, iron and steel, armaments and textiles. Most of these were in the Czech lands, though Slovakia had some mining and metal smelting. The economic development had been matched by social development. The people were as a whole educated, politically aware, and tolerant. It was symptomatic of the country that its national minorities were the best treated in eastern Europe. For example, by 1927 there were 39 Slovak grammar schools for secondary education beyond the age of 14; in 1918 there had been none. The Czechoslovak state in fact was the only new state where a democracy was established and continued to function effectively through the whole inter-war period. It was finally brought down by external not internal forces. Thomas Masaryk, elected as the first President in 1920, remained a symbol of the new republic's belief in moderate reform and justice.

Thomas Masaryk

The German minority

The exception in eastern Europe

The success of the state did not mean there were no problems to overcome. The industries of Bohemia and Moravia were cut off from their previous markets in the empire by the new frontiers. They relied on exporting and were badly affected by the economic crises in Germany and Austria in the years after the war, and also by the raising of the tariff barriers by their neighbours. Timber exports from Slovakia and Ruthenia to their traditional Hungarian market were similarly affected.

Czechoslovakia enjoyed a prosperous period in the middle 1920s as did much of Europe. By 1929 her industrial output had risen 40% above its pre-war levels and her engineering, aircraft and automobile industries did especially well. The Skoda armaments and heavy engineering works were world-famous, and so too was the shoe-making firm of Bata. The people enjoyed a highly developed system of social services. Land distribution laws, which broke up the very large estates, eased the land hunger and lessened class differences.

The problem of
the minorities
But the country was very badly hit by the depression; by 1933 one-third of the population was without an earned income. Ruthenia and Slovakia were very much affected by the drastic fall in agricultural prices and the raising of tariff barriers by Hungary. The industries which relied on exports collapsed. Unfortunately, the hardest hit areas were also those with the national minorities. The Ruthenians and Slovaks have already been mentioned; the Germans were also hard hit. They were very active in the light industries of textiles, glass and ceramics, and they greatly depended on exports to Germany, Austria and the West which collapsed in the early 1930s. Movements for greater self-rule grew in size, fuelled by the economic discontent and encouraged by outside enemies. A small German-based Nazi Party, led by Konrad Henlein, although initially banned, survived and became more extreme. It was soon taking orders from Berlin. An extreme Slovak Nationalist Party led by a Roman Catholic priest, Father Hlinka, also gained in strength. This looked for encouragement first to Hungary but also later to Nazi Germany. Neither group, however, won majority support even in its own area.

Benes
Czechoslovak foreign policy had recognized the precarious independence of the new countries of central and eastern Europe. Eduard Benes, who was the Czech Foreign Minister and then President on Masaryk's retirement in 1935, had been an active participant in the League. The Czechs hoped for co-operation among the small states and even suggested an economic federation. This failed to materialize and the main planks in Czech diplomacy were the 'Little Entente' with Romania and Yugoslavia, against the Hungarian revisionist ambitions, and an alliance with France signed in 1924. The rise of Nazi Germany posed a major threat and a mutual aid treaty was signed with Soviet Russia in 1935, allowing for help under attack, providing France too honoured her commitments under a similar agreement.

The destruction
of
Czechoslovakia
In 1938 Henlein was ordered by Hitler to demand full autonomy (self-rule) for the Germans — now known as the Sudeten Germans, from the Sudetenland area they lived in (CORE, pp. 49–50). Britain and France, instead of supporting the Czechs, ordered them to come to terms with Henlein's Nazis and then with Hitler, when he demanded the incorporation of the Sudeten Germans in the German Reich. The Czechs felt betrayed and

many of the army leaders urged President Benes to fight. With no foreign support forthcoming he declined to do so, and half of Bohemia, with most of the Czech fortifications and industry, came under German rule in October 1938. Benes resigned and went into exile in Britain. The state ceased to exist in March 1939 when Hitler occupied the rest of Bohemia and Moravia. Slovakia became officially independent under German 'protection'; Ruthenia was returned to Hungary.

Part III
Russia since 1945

8

Stalin's Russia (IV)

(1) The Cold War

Potsdam and the quarrel over eastern Europe By the time the Big Three met again, at Potsdam in July 1945, the war in Europe was won, Roosevelt had died and Churchill had been removed from power after his defeat in a general election. The Big Three were now Stalin, Prime Minister Attlee, and President Truman. Relations between the Allies had soured considerably, and the main cause was the problem of eastern Europe. As Russian troops 'liberated' the area from Nazi rule Stalin had installed Communist regimes. His action in Poland, where he had refused to keep to the Yalta formula, was especially resented in the West, for Britain and France had entered the War in 1939 in order to defend Polish freedom. Stalin pointed out that twice in recent history Russia had been invaded by Germany through Poland, and Russian security now demanded that she be made into an effective buffer by being Russian-dominated. Some agreement was possible on other issues. Germany and Berlin, Austria and Vienna, were each divided into four zones of occupation, one each for the USSR, America, Britain and France (CORE, pp. 78–9). An Allied Control Commission was established to co-ordinate the administration of the defeated German Reich. Poland's western border was moved further west and fixed along the Oder and Neisse rivers; this compensated Poland for the lands Russia took from her in the east. The German minority was moved into Germany, as were the Germans in Czechoslovakia, Hungary, Romania, and Yugoslavia. They were not to be left as a potential grievance to ruin international stability in the future. Russia also agreed to enter the war with Japan. This, however, proved militarily unnecessary as the Americans brought about the Japanese surrender by dropping atom bombs on Hiroshima and Nagasaki. Nevertheless, Russian troops entered Manchuria and North Korea before the final

The division of Germany

Russia enters war with Japan

Two cartoons on the Cold War — 'Promising pupil' (*above*) and 'Just pasting Stalin's head over my pre-war cartoons. Saves time!' (*below*)

surrender was agreed. Stalin showed no outward alarm at the USA having such a deadly weapon in her arsenal, but it must have worried him as relations became increasingly strained. Soviet scientists were set to work to produce a Russian version at top speed, and they succeeded in their task by September 1949.

Russian domination of eastern Europe

With the war over, Stalin ordered the removal of raw materials, machinery, even whole factories and work-forces from the occupied countries to assist in the rebuilding of Russia. He also made sure that the fairly broad-based governments in eastern Europe were relentlessly narrowed down until all non-Communist opposition had been removed. The last state to go completely Communist was Czechoslovakia in 1948 (p. 139), the one central European state to have survived as a democracy between the wars. Stalin pursued this policy for security reasons. Russia had been invaded from the West in 1914, during the Civil War, and again in 1941. Stalin, as all Communist leaders before and since, pointed out that the West had been hostile to the Communist state since its birth, and he wanted a buffer of 'friendly' states along Russia's border as a form of protection. Any capitalist government would be hostile, so 'friendly' meant 'communist'. Between the wars the West had used the central European states as a buffer against Russia. Stalin now reversed this. Poland, Hungary, Romania, Bulgaria and Czechoslovakia became satellites of Moscow. They were linked to Russia by defence treaties and their economies were so organized as to be of maximum benefit to the Soviet Union. They were forbidden to receive American aid under the Marshall Plan, which Stalin feared would lead to American interference. In 1949 they were all linked together in the Council of Mutual Economic Aid, or *Comecon*, which was to co-ordinate their future development (CORE, p. 87).

The break with Yugoslavia

The one Communist country which refused to bow to Stalin's will was Yugoslavia, where President Tito, the former Partisan leader, opposed Moscow's interference and its plans to turn the country into a second-rate agricultural nation (p. 136). Stalin raged and threatened, 'I shall shake my little finger and there will be no Tito'. He expelled Yugoslavia from *Cominform*, the revived *Comintern*, and imposed an economic blockade. Tito, however, survived, thanks to his popularity within his own country and Stalin's hesitation about actually waging war. As a result of Tito's defiance alleged sympathizers were rounded up in the other east European states and a series of purges and executions followed.

Russia's former allies watched these events with increasing concern. Stalin was sealing off eastern Europe from the West and making it part of the Communist world. Winston Churchill described the situation in a speech at Fulton, Missouri in 1946, saying: 'From Stettin in the Baltic to Trieste in the Adriatic an Iron Curtain has descended across the continent.' There was little the West could do, short of starting another war, since Russian troops were actually in occupation of those countries. But they made it quite evident that they regarded this red menace as equal to that of the recently defeated Hitler. Certainly they determined to resist any further Communist advance — whether at the Dardanelles Straits from the Black Sea into the Mediterranean, which Russia wanted to control jointly with Turkey, or in Greece, where a Communist-led revolt against the monarchy was taking

The 'Iron Curtain'

place. The Amercian policy of containing communism was announced in the Truman Doctrine of 1947 (CORE, p. 83), and it was strengthened by the formation of NATO in 1949 (CORE, p. 86). Stalin considered that the West's attitude showed no regard for Russia's need for security. Why, if the West had spheres of influence, should Russia behave otherwise? He replied to the Truman Doctrine by forming the Communist Information Bureau, or *Cominform*, which was dedicated to organizing revolution and co-ordinating the actions of the world's Communist Parties. Relations between Russia and the West became so frosty that 'Cold War' was said to have broken out (CORE, pp. 81–3).

The Berlin blockade and the division of Germany
Given this atmosphere of distrust there was little hope for co-operation over the future of Germany, despite the Potsdam agreement. There was certainly no chance of a reunion since neither the East nor the West could risk the possibility of Germany falling under the other's influence. With the division becoming increasingly permanent Stalin attempted to get the British, French, and Americans out of their sectors of Berlin in 1948. The old German capital was right in the middle of the Russian zone, so he sealed off all land communication between the city and western Germany. The Western powers were, however, in no mood to give way and the Berlin airlift of supplies kept their zones supplied with essentials until Stalin gave way in May 1949 (CORE, pp. 83–5). The Western powers then merged their zones in western Germany into a new Federal state. In reply, the Soviet Union formally established the Democratic Republic of Germany in her zone.

The Cold War in Asia
The Cold War was not confined to Europe. In Asia Russia gained a somewhat unexpected Communist ally. Few people had anticipated a Communist take-over in China and Stalin had certainly given little aid to Mao and his followers (AA, pp. 68–9). However, he naturally welcomed the declaration of the Communist People's Republic of China in October 1949, and Mao soon visited Moscow. A formal alliance was signed in 1950; Russia gave up her control of the Manchurian railway and Port Arthur, which she had regained in 1945, and promised considerable aid. It remained to be seen whether Mao would bow to the will of Stalin.

The Korean War
A few months later the Russian-backed Communist government of North Korea, which had been left behind when Russian troops withdrew in 1948, launched an attack on South Korea, in an attempt to unify the country under their control (CORE, pp. 132–3, 150–151). Russian absence from the Security Council, in protest over the Chinese seat at the UN being retained by the Chinese Nationalists, allowed the United States to gain UN support for action to contain the Communist threat. A bitter struggle followed and an armistice was only signed in July 1953, by which time Stalin was dead and buried.

(2) **Russia at Home 1945–53: Recovery, Expansion, and Repression**

Russia emerged triumphantly victorious from the war. But her losses had been enormous. Probably 20 million of her inhabitants had perished; vast tracts of land had been devastated by war; factories, houses, railway lines and power stations had been wrecked. According to official statistics 1710 towns and 70 000 villages had been destroyed along with 32 000 industrial enterprises and 64 000 kilometres of railway track. In these circumstances the Soviet leaders immediately launched a recovery programme and demanded further sacrifices from their people. A fourth Five-Year Plan was formally adopted for the years 1946–50, and this envisaged not simply a return to the pre-war situation but expansion on a large scale. As in the earlier Plans, industry was the first priority; basic consumer goods, such as clothing and shoes, were relegated once again to an inferior role.

The Fourth Five-Year Plan, 1946

By 1950 total industrial production had increased about 48% over the 1940 figures, the greatest success coming in metals, coal, oil, electricity output and in the production of tractors. There was a concentration on what was known, on reaching target figures in well-tried ways; by contrast there was a lack of investment in the new fields of chemicals, plastics, and natural gas. Most consumer goods failed to reach even their limited output targets; thus, although industrial wages increased, there were few comforts for the workers. Housing too, despite massive rebuilding programmes, remained desperately short.

Industry

Recovery in agriculture was less marked. The area under cultivation during the war had dropped drastically, and much of the best agricultural land had been under German occupation. The post-war shortages were depressingly serious; farm buildings, equipment and livestock had been decimated and the manpower shortage in the villages was worse than in the towns. The new Five-Year Plan was meant to increase production well beyond that of 1940. Yet agriculture was kept very short of investment; moreover, the traditional Stalinist policy of harsh rule for the peasantry continued. To make matters even worse, 1946 saw possibly the worst drought in modern times: the grain harvest was a quarter below even the appallingly low yield of 1945.

Agriculture

During the war central control over the collectives had of necessity been relaxed and private holdings had increased in size. In 1946 the government decreed that all lands lost to the *kolkhozes* had to be recovered. The peasants were expected to produce more, despite the fact that the state prices paid for their produce did not rise, whereas taxes did. The collectives were made responsible for providing seed formerly distributed by the ministry, and they were supposed to set aside more money for investments in projects, such as forest planting to prevent soil erosion. In 1949 an order for a great expansion of livestock and dairy production was issued, yet the prices for the produce were very low. It is little wonder that agriculture remained depressed and that some collectives were reduced to a state of abject poverty. The *kolkhozes* which did best were those growing crops for industry such as cotton, or those near large towns, where there was a ready market for the produce grown on the private plots. With so many demands and so little investment or incentive provided, 1950 agricultural production in general, and the grain harvest in particular, failed to reach even the relatively low levels of 1940.

Collectives — incentives and investment missing

In his public pronouncements after the war Stalin recognised the immense sacrifices the Soviet people had made and he congratulated them on their victory. A relaxation of government and party control was expected by many. But despite his official speeches Stalin remained intensely suspicious of his people, always assuming their loyalty could best be secured by harsh

Repression continued

rule and threats. Returning prisoners of war were regarded as virtual enemy collaborators and many found themselves exchanging a German prison camp for a Russian one. Russia's Western allies forcibly returned many Russian exiles who had no wish to go back, and evidence suggests that many of these people were shot.

'Russian superiority'

Russian patriotism had been fostered during the war and the greatness of the Russian people, as opposed to the other Soviet nationalities, was now repeatedly stressed. This soon became a narrow Russian nationalism, proclaiming Russian superiority in all fields of human activity. Russians, it was claimed, had invented most things of great importance, from the steam engine and penicillin to the radio and aeroplane. Western life was inferior and lacking in morality and all contacts with Western 'cosmopolitanism' were cut. Marriage between Soviet citizens and foreigners was forbidden. In

Control of the arts

charge of cultural matters until his sudden death in 1948 was Andrei Zhdanov, who had been associated in the 1930s with the advent of 'socialist realism'. He continued to keep a strict control of the arts and demanded that they serve the state. Russia's top composers, Prokofiev and Shostakovich, were expected to turn out trivial folk melodies which appealed to the average official. State interference went into the sciences as well; state scientist Lysenko denied the existence of chromosomes and genes in the human body and this became 'official policy'. Stalin himself wrote an essay on linguistics in 1950. He wished to be revered not simply as a ruler, but also as a man of infinite wisdom and knowledge.

Anti-Semitism

Anti-Semitism was another feature of the last years of Stalin. The Communists had always prided themselves on their lack of racial prejudice, and officially continued to do so; but now Jews found themselves under increasing attack, usually labelled as 'rootless cosmopolitans' or Zionists (people who favoured a Jewish State in Palestine). Russia had in fact voted for the establishment of a Jewish State in 1948, but this seems to have been simply to encourage a British withdrawal from the Middle East. In early

The 'Doctors' Plot'

1952 a 'Doctors' Plot' was revealed, in which nine top doctors, six of whom happened to be Jewish, were accused of having plotted with the United States through a Jewish charity organization to medically ill-treat and murder high-ranking Soviet officials. The sudden death of Zhdanov was attributed to them. Many people suspected that another great purge was

Stalin lying in state

Death of Stalin, 1953

about to be unleashed. Before this could happen Stalin himself suffered a stroke and died on 5 March 1953. He was buried a few days later alongside Lenin in the mausoleum in Red Square.

(3) Stalin — an Assessment

Stalin had ruled Russia for a quarter of a century. Most Russians could not remember a Russia without him. This was a remarkable achievement for a man whose early life and qualities could not have suggested any such future. But what were the effects of his rule on the Soviet Union?

Stalin had come to power in a country which was just recovering from the disasters of war and revolution, a basically agricultural country with a great potential, but lagging behind much of the developed world. He left behind him in 1953 a highly industrialized nation with an output second only to that of the USA. The Soviet people were educated and served by a high standard of medical and social services. Russia was now one of the world's two super-powers. She had not only survived the onslaught of Nazi Germany but had played a major part in the defeat of that nation. Lands lost by imperial Russia in 1904–5 and by Bolshevik Russia from 1918 to 1921 had been regained, and the USSR now dominated large areas of the world from East Germany and Czechoslovakia in the west to North Korea in the east. She had gained an ally, as yet unpredictable, in Communist China. The successes were undeniable, but so too were less attractive features of Stalin's rule.

Industrialization had been achieved at a vast human cost, probably a far higher cost than that of Britain's industrial revolution. This was mainly the result of the break-neck speed that was insisted upon, for reasons of national security. There had also been vast failures. The collectivization of agriculture had been brutal and to little effect economically. It had failed to increase production and therefore could not finance Russia's industrialization, which instead was paid for by a drastic drop in the living standards of ordinary people. There was probably no other way in which it could have been done so very quickly. In many characteristics Stalin is reminiscent of the Tsars Ivan the Terrible and Peter the Great, who were violent, energetic and remorseless tyrants, but now well represented in the new Russian history books. He had great ambitions both for himself and Russia, and an almost total disregard for the individual within the cause. He was prepared to use force and terror to eradicate all opposition and extreme brutality to drive the Russian people to do his bidding. What marks him out from the Tsars is the cause that he championed, the cause of world communism. All that was done was supposedly for the benefit of the workers and was with their co-operation. Where this was not forthcoming the powers of the state and party were used to compel them. Stalin in fact put to 'good use' the less attractive features of the Soviet state that had been developing during Lenin's lifetime. There was also born the 'big lie'. Collectivization was presented as a voluntary movement of highly aware and socially-minded peasants, which proceeded well after the richer peasants, the kulaks, had been removed. The standard of living of the people was said to be improving in the mid 1930s, when in fact it was dropping drastically. Setbacks and failures (which were bound to occur) were hidden behind false statistics, ignored, or treated as sabotage.

At the centre of the official picture of the Soviet Union was the infallible Stalin, the wise philosopher leader, the worthy successor to the great Lenin, whose devotion to the Russian people and world communism knew no bounds. In reality the situation was rather different. Stalin quite evidently distrusted the ordinary people and seemed to have little faith in the very creed he was expounding. The enthusiasm and revolutionary fervour had disappeared. Debate had given way to orders, discussion to the official party line. A symptom of this was the destruction of the party intelligentsia in the purges of the 1930s, and its replacement by a bureaucracy and obedient officials who offered no threat to Stalin's power.

In foreign affairs, despite great successes, there had also been bad mistakes, above all the failure to recognize the danger that Hitler's rise to power might pose and the need to organize to prevent it. Similarly, Stalin ignored all the evidence which was presented in 1941 to suggest that Hitler was about to break the Nazi-Soviet pact, and Russia suffered disastrous defeats as a result. In fact Stalin's foreign policy was very similar to that of Tsarist Russia, emphasizing Russia's national needs and aspirations. The imposition of Communist regimes in eastern Europe in 1945 smacked very much of empire-building of the sort that Marxists had always condemned in others.

In Western eyes Stalin's very real achievements are recognized, but he stands condemned for his brutality and total disregard of individual freedom. He also stands condemned because of what followed him. Had the less pleasant aspects of Soviet life under Stalin been removed in subsequent years his rule might have been seen as a necessary, if unfortunate stage, in Russian development. As they remain, if in a somewhat less brutal form, Stalin is seen as a tyrant who transformed the Soviet Union into the totalitarian state it remains today.

9

Soviet Russia under Khrushchev

(1) De-Stalinization and the Secret Speech of 1956

Collective leadership

Stalin had so dominated the party and government that on his death in 1953 there was no one with the standing or power to rule alone. A period of collective leadership followed, with four main figures involved: Malenkov, Beria, Molotov, and Khrushchev. Georgi Malenkov was probably Stalin's choice as the new leader, and he had made the major speech at the 19th party Congress just before Stalin's death. An intelligent man, who had made his mark by service to Stalin in the party secretariat, he lacked qualities of leadership. Lavrentii Beria, like Stalin a native of Georgia, was the renowned and feared head of state security and Minister for Internal Affairs. Vyacheslav Molotov, Prime Minister in the 1930s, and later Foreign Minister, was one of the few old Bolsheviks to have survived. Finally, there was Nikita Khrushchev, who had risen as a loyal servant of Stalin in the Ukraine and had become a member of the Politburo in 1939. His chief interest was agriculture. Since 1949 he had been working within the party secretariat and was also First Secretary in the Moscow party. His direct manner, cheerfulness and slight unpredictability, which many associated with his peasant background, made him appear a less than likely candidate for the leadership.

The struggle for power

Beria removed . . .

Malenkov now became the new Prime Minister and main spokesman for the government, but he was forced by the others to give up his position in the secretariat to prevent him being too powerful. This left Khrushchev as Chief Secretary. Beria kept charge of security and internal affairs, Molotov foreign affairs. A new more relaxed mood was soon in evidence. The government declared an amnesty for the thousands of prison camp inmates and admitted that the Doctors' Plot had been a pack of lies. Malenkov promised the Soviet people a better life with more consumer goods and considerable aid to the farming population. He also called for a relaxation in tension with the Western world. On the surface the entire government appeared to be in favour of these policies; yet behind the scenes there was already a struggle for power. Khrushchev began to use his position within the party to appoint his own followers to important posts and committees. Moves were made to dismantle Beria's huge security empire which had been outside the party's control and answerable only to Stalin. Then in July it was suddenly revealed that Beria had been removed from all positions of authority and expelled from the party. He was accused of attempting to use the powerful security system and Ministry for the Interior to seize power, as well as a host of other crimes, such as trying to undermine

Russian agriculture and being a foreign spy. A few months later (in December 1953) he and some of his associates were tried in secret and executed.*

... and
executed

New measures to ensure 'socialist legality' were now introduced. The powers of the police to arrest without a warrant and imprison without a trial were severely restricted and the system of justice was improved. Confessions of the accused were no longer to be sufficient to lead to conviction, and crimes against the state were to be tried in public. These reforms were soon followed by further amnesties which freed most of the prison camp population, and conditions were improved for those who remained. In Soviet life there was something of a 'thaw', so called from a book with that title which advocated a relaxation of controls. Books and plays appeared which were critical of certain aspects of the Soviet system, such as its huge bureaucracy. Other works departed from 'noble' themes and concerned themselves with human emotions and crises. Contacts were renewed with the West and cultural and scientific exchanges took place. A few foreign tourists began to appear in Soviet cities and travel for Russians abroad became a possibility. The law forbidding marriage between Soviet citizens and foreigners was repealed.

Police powers
reduced

The 'thaw'

There were, however, strict limits. Open criticism of the government or of Marxism was still impossible, and artists could have their lives made a misery. The famous Russian composer Shostakovich was forced to apologise for his Tenth Symphony and Boris Pasternak was compelled to turn down the Nobel Prize for literature that was offered to him in 1958. His book on the Russian Revolution, *Dr Zhivago*, had been published abroad, but was not allowed past the censors at home. Religion was again discouraged. Khrushchev later became one of the greatest persecutors of the Church, closing down thousands of churches between 1959 and 1964. Many synagogues suffered a similar fate and thousands of people were taken to court for spreading religion amongst the young.

Persecution of
the Church

Stalin's reputation as the infallible leader was gradually undermined. *Pravda*, the official party newspaper, attacked individual rather than collective leadership, and Stalin ceased to appear as Lenin's right-hand man in the new edition of the history of the Communist Party. In December 1953 there was no reference to the former leader's birthday. But all this was nothing compared to the onslaught that was unleashed in 1956. The 20th Party Congress met that February, and in a secret speech, with all foreign delegates excluded, Khrushchev proceeded to attack Stalin in the most devastating fashion. The former leader was accused of having built up 'the cult of the individual', glorifying himself as a 'superman possessing supernatural characteristics akin to those of a god'. This was held to be quite at variance with Marx's views and the way in which Lenin had behaved. Its most harmful result was the power which Stalin had accumulated and used in a totally unscrupulous way, and which doomed all opposition to 'moral and physical annihilation'. Lenin's last testament — in which he had expressed his concern at faults in Stalin's character and suggested his replacement by someone more suitable — was now read. Khrushchev then

The secret
speech of 1956

---

* His entry and photograph in the *Great Soviet Encyclopaedia* were replaced by a new entry on the Bering Sea.

Khrushchev making his 'secret speech', 1956

began to detail the main abuses of power of which Stalin was held to have been guilty, and he concentrated on the purges of the 1930s. He explained how many totally innocent people had been arrested and later imprisoned or executed. 'Honest Communists' had been the victims, for by that stage the Trotskyists and enemies of the revolution had been defeated and 'the revolution was already victorious'. A good example was the fate of the delegates chosen for the 1934 Party Congress, the so-called 'Congress of Victors'. Of the 1966 delegates elected, 1108 had been arrested; of the members of the party's Central Committee, 70% had been arrested and shot by 1938. The prisoners had been tortured and made to sign false confessions to enormous crimes. A mass terror had been unleashed on Russia and Khrushchev made it clear that it had all been done on Stalin's orders. He had not simply been misled by officials, although 'Beria's gang' had been guilty accomplices in the whole ghastly procedure.

Khrushchev declared that Stalin had also not been the genius he had liked to proclaim himself. He had been blind to the obvious, that Hitler's Germany would at some time attack Soviet Russia, and he had failed to take notice of the many warnings that had been given of the date of the attack. These faults, together with his failure to prepare the USSR adequately by producing sufficient weapons and ammunition, had led to disaster. Not content with that, Khrushchev continued that Stalin was:

> interfering with operations and issuing orders which did not take into consideration the real situation at a given sector of the front and which could not help but result in huge personnel losses.

His purge of the armed forces in the 1930s had also unnecessarily weakened Soviet military strength. In his self-glorification he took all credit for the victory as if he had made all the plans, and down-graded officers, such as Marshal Zhukov, who could claim some of the glory. This falsification of history had continued in an extreme fashion after the war; Khrushchev presented a picture of Stalin heaping extra praise on himself in the official Communist Party history by adding comments in the margin of what had so far been prepared for publication. In the post-war years the poor relations with Yugoslavia had been Stalin's fault, and he had 'completely lost consciousness of reality' in his 'mania for greatness'. The last example of this was the Doctors' Plot, which was 'fabricated from beginning to end'.

The attack on Stalin made in this speech was completely damning and very extreme. It was a bombshell, the more remarkable in view of the hero-worship of the great Stalin that had been current for so long. Khrushchev was, however, careful to extricate the party from any blame. He wished to avoid the obvious implication that something was wrong with a system that allowed such things to take place. The party was praised:

> Our historical victories were attained thanks to the organizational work of the Party . . . and to the self-sacrificing work of our great nation . . . and were not at all the fruit of the leadership of Stalin, as the situation was pictured during the period of the cult of the individual.

Khrushchev also had to explain what the members of the party and government had been doing at that time, and why they had not opposed Stalin; for the present leadership had made its way up during the Stalin era. The explanation was that they had had to support Stalin in his struggles with the followers of Trotsky, Zinoviev, and Bukharin to ensure the correct policy was adopted; after that they had been powerless and those who had tried to intervene had themselves become victims of the terror.

The delegates were asked to keep the speech secret but it soon leaked out, and the American State Department published an accurate account in June 1956. The down-grading of Stalin continued with the renaming of hundreds of streets, canals, collectives, schools and towns. Stalingrad, for example, became Volgograd. Finally, in 1961, his body was removed from the Lenin Mausoleum and buried alongside lesser Communist figures beneath the Kremlin walls. *

---

*On the single occasion when publication of a book highly critical of the government was allowed, it was an attack on the prison camp system under Stalin. This was Alexander Solzhenitsyn's *One Day in the Life of Ivan Denisovitch*. Khrushchev overruled the censors to get it published in 1962.

(2) Khrushchev's Rise to Supremacy

By the time of the secret speech Khrushchev had increased his importance considerably. He had used the right-wing of the party and the military to bring down Malenkov for advocating the build-up of consumer goods. It was felt that this would lead to a lessening of Russia's industrial base and military power. So Malenkov had resigned in February 1955 and his post as Prime Minister was taken by Nikolai Bulganin, a figurehead. Power lay with Khrushchev, who now increasingly brought his followers into the secretariat, the Central Committee and the Politburo, or Presidium, as it was known after 1952.

Attempts to remove Krushchev

He soon had to face a new challenge. Many party members were critical of the slightly freer atmosphere in Russia and had not approved of the attack on Stalin. In particular, they blamed Khrushchev for the troubles in eastern Europe that seemed to follow the secret speech during 1956. The rehabilitation of leaders imprisoned by Stalin had also led people in the satellite states to believe that they could remove Stalinists from power and pursue policies freer from the control of Moscow. Serious outbreaks of violence had occurred in Poland, (see p. 126), which had led to a new government and concessions from Moscow; and in Hungary, a full-scale revolt had required a large Russian military operation to put it down (see p. 131). The attack on Khrushchev came in 1957 and the occasion was a debate on economic planning. Khrushchev was outvoted by seven to four in

Khrushchev triumphs

the Politburo, but by cleverly mobilizing his supporters he got a special meeting of the Central Committee of the Party to overrule their decision. His opponents were forced to resign. In 1958 he forced out Bulganin too, and himself took over the post of Prime Minister, thus occupying the top positions in both the party and government. Henceforward, until his fall in 1964, he was the real ruler of Russia, although he could never ride roughshod over his colleagues as Stalin had. He did not have this amount of power mainly because he could not use, and probably did not wish to use, the state security system in the same way. One sign of a new atmosphere was the fact that the ousted leaders were not arrested and shot. Instead they were found posts of little political importance. Malenkov, for example, was Minister of Electric Power for several years.

(3) Agriculture, Industry and Living Standards

Agriculture was one of Nikita Khrushchev's major interests and, even in 1953, he was the main spokesman on agricultural affairs. His early policy statements stressed the depressed nature of Russian agriculture, which had previously been hidden behind false statistics, and he pointed the way to remedies. These were to be greater investments, higher prices for agricultural produce to give the farmer an incentive to grow more, and the

Aid for agriculture

training of skilled personnel to produce more scientific farming methods. 'Procurement' prices were raised at once. Procurement was the amount the state required as a compulsory delivery, most noticeably for grain where the price was increased seven times, and for beef where the increase was five-fold. The procurement quota was cut to allow more to be sold on the open market. Taxes on the private plots were cut by nearly a half, farmers owning no livestock were freed from a compulsory delivery of meat to the state, and tax deduction encouraged the purchase of an increased number of animals. Collective farm debts to the state were written off. These concessions helped to double production in two years.

The 'virgin lands' scheme   In 1954 Khrushchev introduced a new venture known as the 'virgin lands' scheme. More grain was needed and the easiest way to produce this was to increase the acreage under cultivation. So huge areas, mainly in southern Siberia and northern Kazakhstan, were to be put under the plough and 150 000 workers, encouraged by the pioneering spirit and financial reward, were to move there to farm and build the necessary roads and houses. It was a gamble, for the areas chosen had long severe winters and were prone to droughts during the growing season. Initially 13 million hectares were sown; the plan was intended to cover 41 million hectares by 1960. Grain production certainly increased, but the figures fluctuated widely according to the weather, and the results were somewhat disappointing. Over-keen or ignorant officials did not leave sufficient land fallow and, as they were growing only one crop, this led to soil exhaustion and erosion. 1963 was considered to be a disaster year, when the harvest was 107 million tons; large quantities of grain had to be imported from Canada. The harvests before and after were better — 140 million tons in 1962 and 152 million tons in 1964 — and these compared well with the 1953–4 average of 83 million tons.

Khrushchev visiting a state farm

Meat and dairy
campaign

Another of Khrushchev's campaigns aimed at increasing the output of meat and dairy produce to a level equal to that of the United States of America. Sowing the virgin lands with grain freed other areas for the growth of fodder crops, especially maize. As with other target figures attached to campaigns, this one tended to get out of hand as local officials and party workers went to extremes in their efforts to please the central authorities. Maize was planted in totally unsuitable areas; some collectives produced more animals than they could feed; others slaughtered so many in one year that they were short in the next.

Khrushchev toured the country on several occasions to see the problems for himself and to badger officials and farm managers to be more efficient and productive. He saw the administration of farming as all-important. Decrees were issued which reduced the power of the Central Ministry of Agriculture and gave local bodies more control over decision-making. In practice there was little improvement, since local party officials interfered in the running of the collective. The peasants resented interference wherever it came from, because it prevented them doing as they wished. This feeling was reinforced when Khrushchev put pressure on them to work harder on the collectives' lands and to hand over their privately owned livestock. He felt that they were concentrating too much on their small private plots, which continued to provide the peasants with an important source of income; they also produced most of Russia's eggs, vegetables and dairy products. The policy of more local control failed to increase production and in 1962 it was reversed with the establishment of a new Central Committee on Agriculture.

Abolition of
MTSs

Another change had taken place in 1958 when the MTSs (Machine Tractor Stations) were abolished and their equipment sold. This suited many collectives which were pleased to own their machinery, but the expense of buying it was too high for some and resulted in a decline in agricultural investment. Some collectives also had problems maintaining their machinery adequately. This change illustrated the main weakness of the Soviet economy. There was no flexibility allowing for varying circumstances. Before 1958 everyone had to hire their equipment; after 1958 no one could.

Industry

Meanwhile, continued industrial expansion remained a top priority. The Fifth Five-Year Plan of 1952, introduced before Stalin died, concentrated again on heavy industry. This was soon reversed by his heirs, who promised more consumer goods to improve everyday life. This shift in emphasis was short-lived and the plans of the Khrushchev era reverted to a concentration on heavy industry, although other goods were not so neglected as they had been during Stalin's lifetime. Khrushchev also tried to build up the newer industries of chemicals, natural gas, and synthetics which had been very short of investment. The plans were as ambitious as ever: indeed the Sixth

The Sixth Plan
abandoned

Five-Year Plan of 1956 was abandoned after one year as unrealistic, although this may have been due to attempts to undermine Khrushchev's position at the time. A Seven-Year Plan was substituted to run from 1959 to

Adoption of
Seven-Year Plan

1965; it was accompanied by a complete change in organization. As in agriculture, Khrushchev felt that there was too much central control which failed to plan or administer adequately the increasingly complex economy of

Central
ministries
abolished

the USSR. The central ministries were abolished and in their place 105 regional economic councils *(Sovnarkhozy)* were established. Gosplan, the central planning committee, was to be responsible for co-ordination. Khrushchev had recognized a very real weakness in the Soviet economy. Yet his solution posed as many problems as it solved. Local councils could not know the needs and resources of the whole country and very quickly they began to concentrate simply on their own areas at the expense of the total

1961 — policy
reversed

economy. In 1961 policy was reversed, 17 area authorities were established to co-ordinate the regions, and in the next two years the number of councils was reduced from 105 to 47. A new Central Supreme Economic Council was created to set targets, and there were three subordinate agencies to organize production. To facilitate party control of the economy the local party organization was divided into two, with one body for agriculture, the other for industry. This led to duplication and confusion. By 1963 the number of organizational changes and different boundaries of administration had become bewildering and no one knew who was responsible for what. Khrushchev said he was planning further changes for 1964!

Achievements in
science and
space

One area of spectacular progress under Khrushchev was the development of science and its use in making military equipment and in space research. The USSR exploded its first nuclear bomb in 1953, fired its first Intermediate Range Ballistic Missile in 1955 and two years later put the first satellite, *Sputnik 1*, into orbit round the earth. This lead over America was maintained when Yuri Gagarin became the first man, and Valentina Tereshkova the first woman, to orbit the earth, in 1961 and 1963 respectively. The USSR was also a world leader in the use of nuclear power for the generation of electricity and had massive skills in physics, applied mathematics, and engineering in particular. Scientific research had been made a top priority and the number of researchers had increased some 20 times since 1928. The achievement was all the more remarkable given the limited education available prior to the Revolution. Developments had in many ways been at the expense of investment in other industries, but industrial production as a whole had increased impressively, especially between 1955 and 1958.

'Communism by
1980'

Successes brought increased optimism and in 1961 a new programme was announced which envisaged the foundations of communism being laid by 1980. By this time it was planned that industrial output per head of population would outstrip even that of the USA. This would necessitate industrial production increasing by 500% and agricultural output by 250%. The state would provide free of charge an expanded system of welfare services, public transport, gas, heating, factory and school meals. There would be a higher standard of living than in any capitalist country and this would ease the transition to the doctrine of 'from each according to his ability, to each according to his need'.

Improved living
standards

Khrushchev earned the gratitude of the average Soviet citizen by the improvements in living standards which took place during his period in office. Wage levels improved with the introduction of a legal minimum wage of 300 roubles a month, while the working week was cut to seven hours a day with six hours on Saturday. At the same time absenteeism and leaving a job without permission ceased to be criminal offences. Tax alterations helped everyone, especially the lower paid, as did the abolition of fees in secondary and higher education which Stalin had introduced in 1940. A vastly improved scheme of disability benefits and old age pensions was introduced with the minimum fixed at the same level as the minimum wage. The acute housing shortage, which had made four families in a four-roomed flat a common feature, was eased by a massive scheme of new housing construction. Medical services improved with an impressive total of doctors and hospital beds available, and vast expenditure on education continued. Education to the age of 15 became compulsory and there was a better staff: pupil ratio than in Britain and the USA.

Modern housing in Moscow

(4) Foreign Policy 1953–64

Relations with the non-Communist world

Stalin's heirs inherited a tense world situation. The Cold War had erupted into fighting in Korea and the Western world was extremely hostile to the USSR and communism. American policy, under the direction of President Eisenhower and his Secretary of State, John Foster Dulles, aimed not only at 'containment' but also if possible at 'roll back', that is, regaining areas 'lost' to communism. As part of this policy the USA constructed military alliances around the two Communist powers and continued to do so after Stalin's death. NATO (created 1949) was joined by the South-east Asia Treaty Organization (SEATO) in 1954 and the Central Treaty Organization (CENTO) in 1955. Russia replied in 1955 with the formation of the Warsaw

The Warsaw Pact, 1955

Pact, a security pact of all the east European Communist states, except Yugoslavia (CORE, p. 87).

The new Soviet leaders made moves to lessen tension. A ceasefire was finally agreed in Korea in July 1953, and Russia was co-chairman 'with Britain of the Geneva Conference of 1954 which attempted to find solutions to the Korean and Indo-Chinese problems. A peace treaty was finally agreed with Austria in 1955. All the occupying powers withdrew leaving Austria a neutral state. Of great significance was Khrushchev's announcement at the

'Peaceful co-existence'

20th Party Congress in 1956 that 'peaceful co-existence' with the capitalist world was possible. The reasons for this change in outlook, which moved away from Marxist-Leninist ideas, were varied. The costs of defence were mounting: military expenditure in the USSR had doubled since 1948, and was by 1955 taking 21% of total state expenditure. Reduced tension could make some of this outlay unnecessary and release funds for the rest of the economy. Perhaps the consequences of a nuclear war were also too much to contemplate. A sign of the new attitude was the travel undertaken by the Soviet leaders in an attempt to make personal contact with other world statesmen. Khrushchev attended the Geneva summit in 1955, visited Britain in 1956, and went to the USA in 1959 to hold informal talks with President Eisenhower.

The German question

In Soviet eyes the main problem with Europe was Germany (CORE, p. 85). No peace treaty had yet been agreed. West Germany had entered NATO in 1954 and was allowed to re-arm, which particularly alarmed the Russians. Berlin was still partially occupied by the Western powers. The question of Germany and European security was discussed at Berlin in 1954 and at Geneva in 1955. The Russians put forward numerous proposals aimed at breaking up NATO in some general agreement on disarmament or on European security, but these failed. Similarly, proposals for a united and neutral Germany got nowhere, as the Russians had no intention of allowing completely free elections in the East. In November 1958 Khrushchev

Crisis over Berlin

provoked a crisis over Berlin, demanding the withdrawal of foreign troops within six months and threatening to take action if they did not leave. He was in effect threatening war, but imagined that the West was so impressed by the launching of *Sputnik* and Russia's advanced missile programme that they would back down. The West called his bluff and nothing happened. Khrushchev demanded another summit meeting, but when it finally met in Paris in 1960 it came to an abortive end. An American U2 spy plane had been shot down over Russia and Khrushchev walked out of the summit. He delivered a swingeing attack on President Eisenhower and his anger revealed itself again in October at the UN, where he attacked Western policies in the Congo and the unsatisfactory structure of the United Nations. The world watched in amazement as, in his anger, 'Mr. K.' banged his shoe on the table (CORE, p. 159). A year later Khrushchev met President Kennedy in Vienna and presented virtually the same ultimatum over Berlin as he had done in 1958. Again the United States refused to back down. The

The Wall Russians then sealed off East Berlin from the Western zones by the building of a huge wall dividing the city, which was then heavily guarded by soldiers. Its main purpose was to stop huge numbers of East Germans fleeing to West Germany via West Berlin (CORE, p. 153).

Interest in the In the 1950s the Russians began to take more interest in the less-developed less-developed nations in Africa, South America, the Middle East and Asia. The USSR had world hitherto concentrated primarily on her own immediate domestic and international position. Now she began to see the possibilities of assuming a role of leadership in the developing countries, by giving aid and supporting them against the old colonial powers. In Asia Russian technical aid and financial credit was given to Indonesia, Burma, and India. Russian delegations visited those countries, and India received Russian diplomatic support in 1962 when the Chinese attacked her border regions. In the Middle East, Egypt, Syria, and Iraq in turn received Russian aid. Egypt did especially well. It was her acceptance of East European armaments that caused the Americans to withdraw aid for the Aswam High Dam (CORE, p. 141), and Russia was then able to step in and offer help with the project. Khrushchev even awarded President Nasser the Order of Lenin, despite the latter's suppression of Egyptian Communists.

Cuba The closest links of all were forged with Fidel Castro's Cuba (CORE, pp. 153–6). When the Americans refused to trade with the island, Mikoyan, Russia's Deputy Premier, went there in 1960 and signed a trade agreement. This enabled the new regime to sell its sugar to Russia and in exchange receive Russian oil. An American-backed invasion of Cuba by anti-Castro exiles, which failed at the Bay of Pigs in 1961, made Castro keen to receive Russian military aid. Within a year Russian missile-launching sites were constructed on the island. Khrushchev had under-estimated American sensitivity at having Russian missiles as close to America as

The Missile American bases in Turkey were to Russia. In October 1962 President Crisis Kennedy received photographic evidence of the launching sites and immediately ordered the Russians to withdraw them. Russian ships carrying missiles were on their way to Cuba and the American President threatened to stop them. Khrushchev at first denied the truth of the evidence and complained about the American bases in Turkey. World tension mounted, and nuclear war suddenly became a very real possibility. Finally, with Kennedy standing firm, Khrushchev backed down. In the following year the two super-powers, realising the dangers of war, established a direct telex

The 'Hotline' link between the Kremlin and the White House, called the 'Hotline', for use and Test Ban in an emergency. They also signed a partial Test Ban Treaty, with Britain Treaty included, outlawing nuclear explosions in the atmosphere, in the sea, and in space. They called on other nations to sign and more than 100 did — with China and France noticeable for their absence.

Relations with After Stalin's death a number of eastern European satellite states the Communist demanded a softening in the hard-line policies upon which he had insisted. states Demonstrations and violence in East Germany led to a slight relaxation there, and reparation payments to the Soviet Union were ended in 1954 (CORE, p. 91). Simultaneously, attempts were made to improve living standards and to remove the most punitive aspects of Communist rule in

Hungary, Romania, Bulgaria, Czechoslovakia and Poland. A closer co-ordination of the economies of the Communist bloc was planned, but little was achieved.

Yugoslavia   As de-Stalinization proceeded relations with Yugoslavia improved. Khrushchev and Bulganin visited Belgrade in 1955, trade links were restored, and economic aid begun. Tito welcomed the new Soviet attitude but was not prepared to bargain over Yugoslavia's national interests; Khrushchev recognized that the two countries could find their own 'different roads to socialism'. De-Stalinization, however, was not without its difficulties as the upheavals in Poland and Hungary in 1956 made clear (pp. 126, 131).

These crises also revealed the limits beyond which Soviet policy would not relax. The east European countries were allowed to take some account of their own national needs. But the eastern bloc security system, the Warsaw Pact, formed in 1955, was not to be weakened; and there was no question of freedom for non-Communist parties.

The break with   The second-ranking Communist power was now China (CORE,
China   pp. 167–8). She was something of an unknown quantity and Sino-Soviet relations were still in a fluid state. Russia had welcomed her new ally, agreed to restore Chinese lands in Russian possession, and promised substantial aid to China's developing economy. The main questions were whether the former national rivalries would continue to be submerged in a united Communist front; and whether the Chinese would be prepared to defer to Moscow's policies as the senior partner in the Communist world. Relations at first remained cordial, but Mao soon became critical of the Russians (AA, pp. 69–70). He could not agree with the Soviet policy of peaceful co-existence with the capitalist world, which Khrushchev had spelled out at the 20th Party Congress in 1956. He considered a war between the capitalist and Communist worlds inevitable, and as Russia developed nuclear weapons and rockets he thought she should use them in this conflict. He seemed to have no fear of a nuclear holocaust, claiming simply that it would bring about the destruction of world capitalism. Mao was also critical of Soviet activities in the Third World, where the Russians were supporting Nationalist, often anti-communist, regimes. This, he said, was putting Russia's national interests first, whereas Communist powers should be supporting the masses in wars of liberation against those very governments. Mao, too, had little sympathy with the increasing manufacture of consumer goods in Russia and the slight easing of Russian rule, when the world Communist victory was yet to be won. Generally he felt that the Russians were going 'soft' and breaking with true Marxism. As well as the ideological differences there were personal elements. Mao had little respect for Nikita Khrushchev, whom he regarded as something of a fool.

The rift between the two countries was concealed for several years behind declarations of unity, but it came into the open in 1960 with the sudden withdrawal of Russian aid and technical advisers from China. Angry attacks appeared in both sides' newspapers. The Russians accused the Chinese of being 'dogmatic', the Chinese denounced the Russians as 'revisionists'. Each said the other was deviating from true communism. The arguments were soon reduced to the level of personal insults. Mao said Khrushchev was a 'psalm-singing buffoon'; Khrushchev retorted that Mao deserved as much respect as a 'worn-out rubber boot'. In 1961 their quarrel flared up over Chinese support for Albania. At the 22nd Party Congress in Moscow Khrushchev attacked Albania's Stalinist policies. Chou En-Lai, the Chinese foreign affairs spokesman, who was in Moscow at the time, rose to Albania's defence. He laid a wreath on Stalin's tomb and abruptly departed for Peking. Russia then broke off diplomatic relations with Albania. In 1962 the Soviet Union declined to support China in her border war with India; China denounced the outcome of the Cuban missile crisis as a Russian sell-out. Such ideological and personal arguments were followed in 1963 by territorial claims, when China demanded the return of lands which had belonged to her in the 19th century and which were now under Russian rule. There were armed clashes along the Sino-Soviet border in November 1963.

(5) Khrushchev's Fall

1963 was a bad year for Khrushchev. The agricultural figures were poor and grain had to be imported, while many livestock were slaughtered for lack of fodder. Some areas were short of food. The last years had witnessed a drop in the growth rate of industry. The upheavals in economic and party organization had made him many enemies and created the demand for a period of stability. In foreign affairs memories of the climb-down over Cuba remained vivid and the conflict with China had split the Communist world. Khrushchev himself appeared to many as undignified and something of a clown in world affairs. His colleagues certainly felt it was time for him to go. The 1964 harvest was good — but came too late to save him. On 16 October *Pravda* announced that Nikita Khrushchev had retired 'in view of his advanced age and the deterioration in the state of his health'. His colleagues on the Central Committee of the party had plotted his fall while he was away on holiday on the Black Sea. Ordered in front of the Committee to explain his mistakes he was forced to resign. He quickly disappeared into obscurity, and when he died in 1971 the only Russian recognition of the fact was a few lines announcing the death on an inside page of *Pravda*.

10
Soviet Russia since 1964

Brezhnev and Kosygin

The years after Khrushchev's fall brought a return to collective leadership in the Soviet Union. The two most prominent members were Leonid Brezhnev, the First Secretary of the Communist Party and Alexei Kosygin, the Prime Minister. Both had risen rapidly as a result of Stalin's purges in the 1930s. Kosygin had become Mayor of Leningrad in 1938, and had since gained a reputation as an able administrator and expert in industrial and economic affairs. Brezhnev had in recent years been responsible for the virgin lands scheme in Kazakhstan and had become a full member of the Politburo in 1957.

Brezhnev, Kosygin and Suslov on the stands of the Lenin Mausoleum

(1) Agriculture and Industry

Attempts to raise agricultural production

The new leaders turned their attention initially to the economic problems that had been a factor in Khrushchev's fall. In agriculture they tried to stimulate greater production by promising less government interference and greater rewards to the farmer. There was to be an end to government campaigns, with their accompanying pressure to meet target figures. Higher prices for produce were introduced. The quota for compulsory delivery to the state was limited, leaving more for private sale if production was high. The private sector, especially in livestock farming, was encouraged by lower taxation, and collective and state farm workers were guaranteed a minimum income and old age pensions. Agriculture had always been neglected as a sector for investment; now large amounts of money were spent on factories

The Kalinin Prospect, Moscow

producing farm machinery, tractors and fertilizers. Such policies, together with the large areas under cultivation as a result of Khrushchev's virgin lands scheme, led to increasing high yields. But the weather inevitably caused great fluctuations. Despite improved policies, the USSR imported large amounts of grain from the USA and Canada — not so much for bread for her increasing population, as for fodder for the livestock industry. This had the disadvantage of using up valuable foreign currency reserves; it also laid the Soviet Union open to political pressure, as was shown in 1980, when the American President Jimmy Carter restricted grain sales in protest at the Russian invasion of Afghanistan.

Soviet agriculture is ceasing to be the great disappointment it was, though there is still much to be done to increase production per worker. Mechanization is still limited: one-third of all agricultural investment under the 1981–5 Five-Year Plan was to be spent on farm machinery and equipment. The young and more skilled workers tend to drift away to the cities, just like their counterparts elsewhere in the world. Over 60% of Russia's population are now city dwellers — despite a marked narrowing in recent years in the gap between the standard of living in the country and that in the towns. To combat this move to urban areas Soviet planners are working towards a merging of state and collective farms and to larger settlements with an increasing number of industries as well as farming. These will provide extra employment and an improved standard of living, and help pay for modern amenities and services.

Industry — central control again

In industry the first changes after 1964 involved a complete reversal of Khrushchev's policy. The central ministries he had abolished in 1957 were re-established to replace the regional economic councils, and the central planning bureau, Gosplan, resumed control of all major planning. The lessening of central control had originally been seen as a way of getting greater local involvement and initiative, which in turn would lead to greater production. Putting the clock back in an attempt to revert to the previous system had obvious dangers. There was talk of experimenting with the freer economic policies being practised in some of Russia's satellite states. The idea would be to release individual companies from so many controls and simply set them a basic target figure and a date for completion. They would be left to decide how to achieve this. But the party administrators fought these ideas, for they had no wish to lose control of the economy; and their view triumphed after the 1968 troubles in Czechoslovakia. The hardliners argued that freeing the economy could easily lead to demands for political freedom; this policy was therefore too dangerous to introduce.

So, despite huge investment, production increases have been limited and target figures often revised downwards. In the early 1980s the Soviet economy remained over-planned, with business initiative suffocated by bureaucrats. Consumer goods were in short supply, especially outside the major cities. Shortages of quite basic products — such as detergents, paint, children's clothing and shoes — were commonplace. The party leaders demand greater efficiency and harder work, but this appears to have little or no effect.

Heavy industry has fared better than those industries producing consumer goods because of greater investment. There have been notable advances as for example, in mineral extraction. The USSR became the largest oil producer in the world in 1974; she now produces about one-quarter of all the world's minerals including oil, coal, iron and phosphates. She has huge untapped resources, though these are often in remote areas which lack housing, transport, and weather reasonable enough to allow extraction. Russian technology is not sufficiently advanced to achieve rapid exploitation of the oil in particular. So the Soviet Union has suffered energy shortages in common with the rest of the world, and has become a competitor for the oil supplies of the Middle East.

Russian technology is generally behind that of the Western world, and the political divisions associated with the Cold War have meant difficulties in obtaining scientific ideas and technological know-how from the West. Better relations between the super-powers mean something more to the Russians than simply lessening world tension and reducing the likelihood of a Third World War. In certain limited areas however, the Russians have concentrated their resources with great success, notably in the space programme of the mid-1960s. They made their first soft landing on the moon in 1970. Arms production, which is dependent on very advanced technology, takes about 13% of total Soviet expenditure, and in this field the USSR is the match of the USA.

The largest oil producer in the world' and *Technology* appear as margin notes.

(2) Stalinism, the Dissidents, and Minority Groups

The fall of Khrushchev halted the anti-Stalin campaign. Brezhnev and Kosygin seemed to favour some kind of rehabilitation of Stalin and it was rumoured that this would take place on the 90th anniversary of his birth in 1969. It did not, apparently because of opposition both from some less hard-line party members and from the eastern bloc Communist leaders. General silence on Stalin's career became the new order, and on the 100th anniversary of his birth in 1979 no official visit was made to his tomb alongside the Kremlin wall. The ordinary people, however, were permitted to lay flowers there.

Brezhnev and Kosygin showed some sympathy with Stalin in their attitude to the arts, where they were stricter than Khrushchev. Completely free expression in the arts or press was not allowed; criticism was regarded as unpatriotic and dangerous, and critics were liable to harassment by the KGB, the state security police, and arrest and imprisonment. Writers and notable figures of the intellectual world became the core of the 'dissident' movement which developed. Its members highlighted faults in the Soviet system, in particular the failure of government to respect individual human rights. Although there was no return to the wholesale terror of Stalin's day, the movement was kept within severe limits. In 1965 two writers, Sinyavsky and Daniel, were sentenced to hard labour for publishing works in the West; others were put into psychiatric hospitals and 'treated' with drugs. Campaigns were organized in the Western world to get certain persons released, to which the Soviet leaders at times gave way, conscious of their world-wide image. Well-known 'dissidents' were also allowed to emigrate or were deported as a means of removing a thorn in the side of the authorities. The most notable example, Alexander Solzhenitsyn, winner of the 1970

Nobel Prize for Literature and author of such books on Soviet prison camps as *The First Circle* and *One Day in the Life of Ivan Denisovitch*, was deported in 1974. Dr Andrei Sakharov, the leader of a group monitoring the 1975 Helsinki Agreement on Human Rights, appeared safe, thanks to world fame as a nuclear physicist and Nobel Peace Prize-winner; but in early 1980 he was deported from Moscow and sent into internal exile at the town of Gorky where contact with the outside world was impossible. Many dissidents were removed from Moscow before the 1980 Olympic Games to prevent them making contact with visitors or perhaps demonstrating and thus spoiling the world's view of the Soviet Union.

National minorities

Opposition to the Soviet regime has come from national minorities such as the Ukrainians and the Lithuanians, the latter being potentially quite strong and closely linked with the persecuted Catholic Church. Religion is still vigorously discouraged as superstition; its practice is severely restricted, and any attempt to teach religion to the young remains an offence. The religious leaders, in an attempt to ensure some kind of survival for their faiths, accepted the regime and avoided political comment. The government then used them as examples of the freedom of conscience allowed in the Soviet Union.

The Jews

Many Russian Jews have striven to retain their separate identity, and have suffered in consequence. A revival of Jewish groups was sparked off by the Israeli victory in the Six Day War of 1967, despite Russian support for the Arab cause. Many Jews dared to apply for exit visas to settle in Israel. At first they were refused and many were harassed by the police. They were helped by the attention drawn to their cause by groups in Britain and the USA, and the rate at which exit visas were granted rose from 400 a year to 33 500 between 1969 and 1973. Those that remained continued to find themselves discriminated against. There has been a very strict limit on the number of Jews allowed into higher education, and the most prestigious institutions, such as Moscow State University, have been closed to them.

Attention has also been given to the Muslim populations of Central Asia, estimated at approximately 50 million in 1980, especially with the religious upsurge in the neighbouring Islamic countries such as Iran. The Asian populations of the Soviet Union are growing at a faster rate than those of European Russia and some commentators have seen a rise in nationalist, religious feeling as a potential threat to the survival of the Soviet state.

(3) Soviet Foreign Policy since 1964

Détente

There was no marked break in Soviet foreign policy as a result of Khrushchev's removal. The policy of peaceful co-existence with the capitalist world that he had first voiced in the mid-1950s was continued. So too were the moves to lessen world tension in the aftermath of the Cuban Missile Crisis of 1962. The 1963 Test Ban Treaty was followed in 1969 by the Nuclear Non-Proliferation Treaty, which aimed to limit nuclear weapons to those powers that already possessed them. The attempt to relax Cold War tensions became known as 'détente', and it gave hope of removing the possibility of a Third World War and a nuclear disaster. Relations with the West, however, were not always cordial. The Russians gave substantial aid to the North Vietnamese in their war against the Americans (CORE, pp. 156-9), and the super-powers had sympathies with opposing sides in the Six Day War in the Middle East in 1967 (CORE, pp. 143-4). The Western powers were alarmed and disgusted by the Russian invasion of Czechoslovakia in 1968 (CORE, pp. 94-5). But they made no move to intervene; the Russian sphere of influence was respected.

The 1970s witnessed further moves to improve East–West relations. A major contribution was the *Ostpolitik* (East policy) of West German Chancellor, Willy Brandt (CORE, p. 160). He gave up German claims to lands east of the Oder–Neisse line and also recognised East Germany as a separate state from West Germany. This led to a four-power agreement on Berlin in 1971, which gave free access to the city and so resolved a long-standing problem. Russia made a number of trading agreements which brought valuable western technology. Among these was a deal settled in 1981, whereby West Germany was to help construct a natural gas pipeline from Siberia, in return for huge supplies of the gas. In 1975 at Helsinki the Western powers agreed to recognize the European boundaries as they had existed since 1945. Russian and Polish gains from that time were accepted and full recognition of the German Democratic Republic re-affirmed. The GDR was already a member of the United Nations Organization. The West was giving little away in recognizing the existing situation, but the Soviet leaders welcomed the recognition of the settlement they had imposed in 1945. A declaration on human rights which all signed gave the West hope that restrictions on individual freedom in the Communist bloc would be lessened; this proved to be misfounded. Soviet agreement with the West was not to be had at the price of interference in Soviet internal affairs.

SALT talks Attempts to stop the fierce arms race between East and West were made through Strategic Arms Limitation Talks (SALT). Beginning in 1969, these also had, and still have, the aim of reducing the huge stockpile of weapons either side already possesses (CORE, p. 161). Only very limited agreements have been reached despite frequent meetings including summit conferences of the leaders of either side. Each side suspects the goodwill of the other. The Russians and their Warsaw Pact allies have continued to spend huge quantities on arms, determined not to negotiate from a position of weakness. Many Western observers fear that the Warsaw Pact forces in Europe are stronger than those of NATO, and that despite their soft talking the Russians are still out to dominate the world and to make the most of any weakness shown by the Western leaders. Certainly the Russians were increasing their world role throughout this period. Their navy appeared in the Indian Ocean and Mediterranean Sea in increasing strength. They continued to be active in Africa. President Sadat expelled the Russian military advisers from Egypt in 1972, but the Soviets found new friends in the Marxist regimes in Angola (CORE, p. 159) and Mozambique. Russia also gave massive support to the Ethiopian government in its war with the Ogaden guerilla fighters backed by Somalia.

The Russians were active too in Asia, giving support to the North Vietnamese government in its invasion of Cambodia at the end of 1978 and challenging China's dominance in the area in the process. In the last month of 1979 and early 1980 a full-scale Russian invasion of Afghanistan took

An increasing
world role

1980 Olympic Games in Moscow

place (CORE, p. 148). Officially it was to help Barbrak Karmal, the new Communist ruler who had ousted a more hard-line Communist rival. The real motivation of the Russians was not at all clear to the Western world at the time. It certainly alarmed the West by bringing Russian forces close to the vital oil supplies of the Persian Gulf. It led to a sudden cooling of relations and attempts by the USA to cut grain exports to Russia. The latter also tried to organize a boycott of the 1980 Moscow Olympic Games, which the Russians were expected to use as a political triumph. Involvement in Afghanistan led to a very difficult war against the hill tribes and many predicted that this would become Russia's 'Vietnam', a war which despite her huge forces and resources she would not be able to win.

Afghanistan — revived tension with the West

Sino-Soviet relations

The new leaders in Moscow in 1964 dropped their verbal attacks on the Chinese; but when this tactic met with no response they soon resumed again. They were very critical of the Chinese Cultural Revolution. The Russian embassy in Peking was subject to a mass siege of Red Guards in early 1967 during which Soviet officials were harassed and abused. In 1968 serious border clashes took place along the Ussuri River; and although the Russians threatened to use nuclear weapons a full-scale war did not follow. Tension later eased and Prime Minister Kosygin visited Peking; yet relations remained very poor even after Mao's death in 1976. Russia continued to support China's opponents, especially the North Vietnamese (CORE, pp. 168–71).

The satellite states

As we shall see, in eastern Europe the satellite states were allowed to pursue policies which did not always follow those adopted in Moscow. Examples included Romania's foreign policy and Hungary's economic development. But there were severe limits to the freedom which they enjoyed. Czechoslovakia learned this in 1968 when a Russian-led invasion ended the attempts of the Czech government to allow greater freedom inside its country (pp. 139–40).

Euro-
communism

One other feature of the 1960s and 70s was the development in western Europe of what came to be known as Euro-communism, that is the independent line taken by the communist parties in that region, especially in France and Italy. Each of these was prepared openly to attack Moscow's policies, especially intervention in Czechoslovakia and Afghanistan. They also said that they would only attempt to obtain power through democratic elections, not through revolution, and that once in power they would allow opposition parties to exist and would respect the electorate's wishes. The Soviet Union did not welcome this split in the European Communist camp, for it might tend to draw the Eastern European Communist Parties away from Moscow.

(4) The USSR in 1981

The Soviet Union in 1981 had come a long way since the Bolshevik take-over in 1917. The USSR was now a vast industrial super-power with a greatly improved standard of living for its people. Everyone was entitled to a job — in fact there was no unemployment — though that does not mean that everyone was efficiently employed. There was an impressive system of education and health care for all. Women had found greater opportunities than ever before and over 90% of the able-bodied went to work, the necessary child-care and schooling being provided. The gap between living standards in town and country had been lessened, especially in the previous 15 years as the farmer achieved greater financial rewards for his work and produce. Yet this rapid development had not been without its problems, nor had it been completely uniform in all areas. In some ways the USSR was still a developing country with transport deficiencies, a chronic housing shortage in the towns, and a lack of consumer goods.

Presiding over the Soviet Union in 1981 was a Politburo of 15 men whose average age was 70. Brezhnev was clearly the dominant figure. Although he had become President in 1977, the incumbent Podgorny being unceremoniously deposed, he had less power than previous leaders. He had, however, achieved a status similar to them and was something of a cult figure. He had become a Marshal and General Secretary of the Communist Party, rather than First Secretary, both titles having last been used by Stalin. On his 70th birthday in 1976 he had been awarded the Order of Lenin and for the second time had been proclaimed Hero of the Soviet Union. The newspapers had printed tributes in glowing terms for seven days. In 1979 he had even been awarded the Lenin Prize for Literature for three volumes of reminiscences.

Brezhnev and Kosygin were both frequently absent from public occasions through ill-health and in October 1980 Kosygin resigned — the only top-ranking Soviet leader ever to have resigned with full recognition of his services. He died in December of that year. His departure made little difference to policy, nor probably will that of Brezhnev when it comes, for there has been a uniformity of outlook in the Politburo. The Russian leaders had nearly all risen under Stalin and were able administrators rather than men of new ideas. They were well aware of the gains that Russia had made, both in the living standards of her people and as a world power. They were also doing very well themselves as representatives of the new ruling class of managers, administrators, and party officials; they had access to decent housing, foreign travel, and a range of consumer goods that the ordinary Russian rarely saw. They wished to preserve what had been achieved; in this sense they had ceased to be revolutionaries and had become conservatives. They feared a relaxation of government control lest this should lead to rapid change and chaos in which all would be lost. There was an obvious lack of freedom of expression and a very limited involvement of the ordinary people in either choosing or running of government. The long Russian tradition of rule from above with limited freedom for the governed had perhaps moulded the country more than the Marxist–Leninists would have liked to imagine. The Soviet leaders, however, failed to admit that there were any shortcomings, and instead continued to suggest that their country represented a model that all should wish to copy.

On the other hand they had perhaps become more realistic in that they ceased to talk in terms of true communism being achieved in the next few years; Khrushchev had predicted in 1961 that the basis of the communist state would be in place by 1980. The newest Constitution, which had been published in 1977, still called the USSR a 'developed socialist state'. The direction of the country by the Communist Party was fully recognized: the party was 'the leading and guiding force of Soviet society and the nucleus of its political system, of all state and public organizations'. There was no reference to the state withering away or to a lessening of central control. *

---

* Leonid Brezhnev died in November 1982 at the age of 75, three days after attending the annual November Revolution celebrations. His place as Party Secretary was taken by the 68-year-old former head of the KGB, Yuri Andropov.

Part IV
Eastern Europe since 1945

11

Eastern Europe since the Second World War

(1) The Soviet Take-over and Communist Policy

The meaning of Communist rule

In the years directly following the Second World War Communist regimes were established in each of the east European states and also in the Russian zone of occupied Germany (CORE, pp. 88–9). With the exception of Yugoslavia and Albania, where the Communist leaders were popular wartime resistance heroes, and to some extent Czechoslovakia, where the Communist Party emerged as the largest single party, these regimes owed their existence to Stalin and the Red Army. At first some share in the government was allowed to other parties than the Communists; but opposition was soon silenced either by the use of intimidation and arrest, or by being merged into the Communist Party itself. 'People's Democracies' were established with constitutional arrangements similar to the Soviet Union. In each, the Communist Party was dominant and, as in the USSR, the most important post was not Prime Minister or President but the First Secretary of the Party. As might be expected, each country also introduced a Soviet economic model with strict central government control, collectivization of agriculture, Five-Year Plans with ambitious targets, and rapid industrialization where this had not yet taken place.

Russian domination

Stalin expected complete obedience from his 'disciples'. He received it because of their total dependence on him for survival. The economies of the 'satellite states' were made to serve Russian interests. Stalin had removed raw materials and even complete factories to the Soviet Union to help Russia's recovery. Those countries that had allied with Hitler were forced to pay reparations, and huge sums were extracted from the Russian zone of Germany. The economies of the satellite states were further exploited by the setting up of joint Russian and local companies which were dominated by

Eastern Europe after 1945

Russians. Equally beneficial to Russia was the policy of buying other countries' goods cheaply and selling her own expensively. The Poles and Czechs wanted to receive Marshall Aid but were prevented from doing so, and the eastern bloc economies were drawn officially into one group by the setting up in 1949 of a sort of eastern European Common Market known as the CMEA — the Council for Mutual Economic Assistance (usually known in the West as *Comecon*). Only Yugoslavia of the People's Democracies did not join; by that time Tito had quarrelled with the Soviet Union by refusing to bow to Stalin's dictates. Yugoslavia had also been expelled in 1948 from the revived Communist International now known as *Cominform* — the Communist Information Bureau — which had been set up in 1947 to co-ordinate the activities of all the European Communist parties (including those in western Europe).

"No, Comrade Stalin! Everyone is out of step except Marshal Tito."

Daily Express Cartoon on uniformity in Eastern Europe from the early 1950s

Following the Moscow line The unequal nature of the partnership between Russia and her allies was further revealed in the way in which their internal affairs were made to reflect events in Moscow. In the years following the Russo-Yugoslav quarrel each country was expected to purge its 'Titoists'. Many prominent Communists were arrested and then imprisoned or executed. Those with Western contacts or a Jewish background were especially suspect. In 1952, to coincide with the Doctors' Plot in Russia, each satellite invented its own 'Zionist' conspiracy against the leadership. The leaders often used these purges to remove rivals, and they became like little Stalins in their own countries. But on Stalin's death in 1953 they had to follow Moscow's example and broaden the leadership. So, in 1956, after Khrushchev's speech denouncing Stalin, each country made some move to get rid of its Stalinists and to admit past errors in government.

'The different roads to socialism'   Even Stalin had been unable to maintain a completely united Communist front in eastern Europe, and Yugoslavia had gone its own way. Khrushchev took a more liberal line, and in his reconciliation with Tito in 1955 he recognized that each country had its own needs; 'different roads to socialism', not just the Moscow one, were possible. At the same time, and partly in response to the change of leadership in Russia, several of the East European leaders began to assert their countries' independence from Moscow. A communist world began to grow up in which the relations between Russia and the separate states were put on a more equal footing. The abolition in 1956 of *Cominform* — which had been used by Moscow to control the other Communist Parties — was one sign of this. Another was the ending of many of the one-sided economic agreements. This step recognized the fact that Communist regimes, which ran their countries merely for the Soviet Union's benefit, were likely to remain very unpopular with their own people. Serious disturbances in the German Democratic Republic in 1953, in Poland in 1956, and a full-scale revolt in Hungary in

The limitation of national freedom   the same year, gave weight to this point. The last also showed how far the independent line could go. There was to be no breakaway from the eastern bloc security system, the Warsaw Pact, established in 1955, and no real freedom for non-Communist parties. When this threatened, Russian troops moved in to restore the situation. The same was to happen in Czechoslovakia in 1968. Russia expected to maintain a special position as leader of the eastern bloc and also to have a final say on anything that threatened the security of the Communist world. The Warsaw Pact treaty, a response to NATO and West Germany's remilitarization within it, was also a means of putting on a permanent basis the right of Russian troops to enter the other member states, all the eastern bloc except Yugoslavia.

Within these limits there was a greater variation in development after the mid-1950s than before. It took several forms. Poland abandoned collectivization; Albania refused to de-Stalinize as Moscow wished; and Romania in the early 1960s refused to co-operate in a CMEA plan, which would have left her as a supplier of raw materials and food for her more industrialized partners. Romania also began to pursue an independent foreign policy and to limit her role in the Warsaw Pact (pp. 132–3). Yugoslavia's freer economy was copied in some aspects by other Communist states, and especially by Hungary, after 1968.

Economic growth   Generally the rate of industrial growth in the Communist states since 1945 has been impressive, especially in the heavy industries and in those countries where there had been little industry before the Second World War. There was less success in those states which were already quite advanced, notably in Czechoslovakia, where the growth rate declined to nothing in the early 1960s. Very strict central control of the economy was not necessarily suitable and was lessened, though in Czechoslovakia itself this trend was reversed after the troubles of 1968. The CMEA also made several useful contributions to economic growth, including the building of oil and gas pipelines to serve its members and the construction of a common electricity grid. Research knowledge has been pooled.

Education and social services   Except in Czechoslovakia, social services and education had been generally underdeveloped before the Second World War. The Communists expanded these to make basic education available to all, and to provide secondary and higher education to large numbers, especially in technology and science. Political education was also considered to be of vital importance. There was also a real attempt to give everyone a reasonable standard of living, to provide decent housing, medical services, old age pensions and the like, and to improve communications so that isolated villages could receive basic necessities and services.

Communist party dictatorship The eastern bloc states have remained dictatorships with limited popular involvement and with no real machinery for changes in government. Leadership changes tend to become major upsets with respectable retirement almost unheard of. Thus individual leaders have tended to remain in power for long periods. By 1980 Hoxha had ruled Albania uninterruptedly since 1945; Tito, who died in 1980, had ruled Yugoslavia for as long. Kadar had been in control in Hungary since 1956; and Zhivkov had been First Secretary of the Bulgarian Communists since 1954. All severely limited the freedom of individuals to criticize the government, although their restrictions on the arts varied considerably — from the hard line of East Germany and Romania, where the arts were made to serve the state, to

Religion Hungary and Poland, which were reasonably liberal. There were great differences, too, in their attitudes towards religion. Initially the Church was persecuted in most of the states and its leaders were arrested. The Church was seen as a supporter of the old social and political order and as having no place in the true Marxist world. In the late 1950s this policy was softened, generally because it failed to work; the persecuted Church was attracting a large following. Instead, a policy was adopted of controlling the Church and getting co-operative leaders. In the more liberal states such as Poland, Hungary, and Yugoslavia, the Church was allowed to operate fairly freely from the 1960s. In others it was barely tolerated, and in Albania simply not allowed.

Most people in eastern Europe have got used to the system under which they live, and are no more critical than the average person in the West. There are, however, in the satellites as in the USSR, a considerable number of intellectuals and writers who resent the lack of freedom. They have become the core of dissident movements, which have tried to bring public attention to this failure. Most people are more concerned with basic living standards which have improved overall, despite shortages of consumer goods. What will happen should standards fall and goods become very short is another question. In 1981 the eastern bloc clearly had severe economic problems — energy shortages, unemployment and predicted 'no growth' in Czechoslovakia, Hungary, and Poland. The troubles in Poland from 1980 plainly showed what could happen (pp. 127-9). The serious unrest there and the establishment of an independent trade union movement, 'Solidarity', which signalled a weakening of Communist Party rule, could have repercussions on the whole eastern bloc. The leaders in other member countries were quick to condemn the 'anti-socialist forces' at work in Poland; and only the Yugoslav and Hungarian press had the courage to tell their readers what the Polish government had actually conceded in their agreements with the Polish workers.

(2) East Germany

Russian
occupation

Russian troops entered Berlin in May 1945, and under the agreements at Yalta and Potsdam the Russians occupied the eastern zone of Germany and the eastern sector of Berlin until a final settlement for Germany could be established. To wartime devastation was now added plundering by the occupying power. Within the first months a huge number of factories in the Russian zone were dismantled and machinery and raw materials removed to the Soviet Union. They were taken officially as reparations, which continued until 1954, by which time their total value had reached some 66·4 billion German marks. The economy was reorganized. A great land distribution was undertaken and over 60% of large-scale industry was either nationalized or taken over by joint Soviet-German, in effect Russian, companies. The Communist Party in Germany, which had existed before 1933, was quickly reformed and its main leaders, Wilhelm Pieck and Walter Ulbricht, were flown in from Moscow. Three other non-Nazi parties were allowed to form as well. The most popular party was the Socialists; but despite their opposition, they were forced to merge with the Communists to form the Socialist Unity Party in 1946. The Communists dominated this.

The establishment of the GDR

With increasing disagreement between the wartime allies, resulting finally in the Berlin Blockade of 1948–9 (CORE, pp. 83–5), it became apparent that German re-unification was no longer possible. So a Communist People's Republic was established in East Germany, known as the 'German Democratic Republic'. Elections from now on, however, gave the electors only one government list of candidates to vote for. The state remained unrecognized by most of the world. It depended for its survival on the USSR, whose troops were very much in occupation.

From 1949 a fully 'socialist' economy was introduced with wholesale collectivization, an end to all private business and trade, and ambitious targets for industrial production. The unpopularity of these measures caused thousands of people to flee to West Germany. Probably some three million left before the Berlin Wall was built in 1961 to stop the flow, and another quarter of a million have gone since. In 1953 the low standard of living and a government attempt to get 10% higher production from the workers for the same pay caused serious outbreaks of violence among the workers in Berlin and several other cities. A general strike was called. A full-scale military operation by Soviet troops was necessary to crush it; many were killed, and 25 000 were arrested. The party leader, Walter Ulbricht, used the opportunity to purge the party of his opponents too. The workers won certain rewards. The new work levels were dropped and pensions increased, but the basic political and economic structure remained as it had been. The economy was helped at that point by considerable financial aid from Russia.

Serious disturbances, 1953

Hard-line government plus economic growth

The East German regime remained very hard-line, not even allowing the publication of certain books printed in the Soviet Union. The government tried to make up for its unpopularity by fast economic growth. The country had considerable natural resources and the economy expanded rapidly. As with West Germany, the recovery from the war years was remarkable. When the growth rate dropped in the early 1960s greater freedom was given to larger businesses to plan, research, and sell as they wished, and expansion then followed. The main industries included engineering, chemicals, ship building, and optical and scientific instrument making. The GDR became Russia's main trading partner, the latter importing half her machinery from there. As the tenth most important industrial power in the world the GDR became a valuable member of the eastern bloc. As elsewhere in the world, the late 1970s brought problems. Here the major one was energy supplies for industry as coal reserves were used up, and imported oil meant running up huge foreign debts. Nuclear power stations were developed as part of the answer.

Under Erich Honecker, who replaced Ulbricht as party leader in 1971, the GDR continued to be the Soviet Union's most reliable ally, exactly following the Soviet line in international affairs. It owed its existence as a separate state to the Russians. Its rulers always feared that a Russian understanding with the West, as part of détente, could lead to them being sacrificed in some united neutral Germany, though any plans for such a move never got off the drawing board. It was only in the early 1970s that the Western world recognized the East German state. West Germany signed a treaty with her in 1972 as part of Brandt's *Ostpolitik* (p. 115) and the GDR entered the United Nations Organization in 1973. As their confidence grew the East German leaders began to cultivate the friendship of several developing countries, especially in Africa.

(3) Poland

Poland, where the Second World War began, was one of the countries most disrupted by it. Partitioned by Russia and Germany in 1939, it was totally occupied by the latter in 1941. Until 1945 it was made to serve the Nazi economy. The Polish people themselves had to submit to Hitler's racial policies; 'inferior' Poles were deported as workers to Germany, German settlers moved in to replace them. Some three million Jews, among them a large proportion of the country's doctors, lawyers, traders and artisans, were exterminated.

The Communist take-over   Stalin had already decided that the Soviet Union would take parts of eastern Poland after the war; Poland was to be compensated by German lands up to the rivers Oder and Neisse. The Allies agreed to this. The question was who was to run the new state. A Polish government in exile with Western support had been established in London, but this was not recognized by the Russians who, on driving the Nazis out, set up a Communist government, based originally on the town of Lublin. Although Stalin promised at Yalta to broaden this government and to allow free elections, the latter were never held. The Government of National Unity that was established was dominated by the Communists under Bierut and Gomulka. Fraudulent elections, which followed the arrest of opponents, apparently confirmed the popularity of the government, but it was in reality a dictatorship imposed from outside, and was therefore deeply resented by the Polish people. Aware of this situation the Polish leaders strictly controlled the political and intellectual life of the country, although the Roman Catholic Church was allowed to survive and even to continue religious education. The government proceeded somewhat cautiously with the socialization of the state. Large-scale industry was nationalized, and heavy industry was built up at the expense of food and consumer goods production. Small private businesses were, however, allowed, and the collectivization of agriculture — though encouraged — was not enforced.

After Stalin's death in 1953 there was a slight relaxation in Poland and those arrested in Stalinist purges were released. Nevertheless, the Church came under attack. Demands for reform were soon heard both inside and outside the government, and matters came to a head in 1956 with serious disturbances in the western industrial town of Poznan. Here the engineering **1956** workers' grievances over wages and conditions soon turned into demands for **disturbances** political change. Gomulka, who had opposed Russian interference in the Polish economy and had been imprisoned in one of the purges as a result, now seemed a suitable leader. He was quickly brought into the government again. With the sudden arrival of an uninvited delegation from Moscow, Soviet military interference seemed a distinct possibility, but realizing that a full-scale national revolt could easily break out the Russians gave way to the 'liberal' line and agreed to allow a more balanced relationship between the two countries. Poland agreed not to follow a separate foreign policy from the USSR — an unlikely move anyway as Polish gains from Germany up to the Oder-Neisse line were rich and her control of these lands depended on Russian support.

Poland under As the new Polish leader, Wladyslaw Gomulka did much to improve **Gomulka** Poland's position. The country had been supplying Russia with huge quantities of coal at a tenth of the world price, and had also had to foot the bill for Soviet troops stationed there. Now these matters were put right; a Polish debt of 2000 million roubles was written off, and new credits were given. The policy of collectivization was abandoned and most of the land passed back into private hands. Most Poles were strong Catholics and an arrangement allowing the Church to function normally was agreed and many of the arrested clergy were freed. There was little alternative, given the hold that the Roman Catholic Church had on the mass of the people. Generally, however, Gomulka turned out to be a disappointment. Greater freedom of speech and the press did not follow; and he rejected as too radical proposed economic reforms, which would have allowed factories and workers considerable freedom from central state control. In practice restrictions were placed on the Church: for example, permission for the building of new churches was often witheld, and a proposed visit by the Pope in 1966 was not allowed. The economy failed to expand, except in agriculture where a reasonable investment level helped to boost production by a third in the early 1960s. Industry was too tightly controlled by government planners and lacked advanced equipment. This was bought in the West in return for Polish food exports, especially meat; yet this led to shortages at home and to discontent. The government had introduced food subsidies in an attempt to keep prices low, but this was ridiculous when food was short. In December 1970, just before Christmas, Gomulka announced price rises of up to 30%. **Gomulka forced** The uproar and strikes that followed in the ports of Gdynia, Gdansk **out** (formerly Danzig) and Szczecin (formerly Stettin) were so serious that Gomulka was forced to resign.

Edward Gierek and economic expansion

He was replaced as First Secretary by Edward Gierek, who — to restore order — now gave considerable increases in wages and welfare benefits and also cancelled the price increases. Gierek then set about getting expansion in the economy, beginning with agriculture. Investment in livestock production, the abolition of compulsory deliveries to the state by farmers, and higher prices for produce helped to stimulate output. The size of farms was increased to achieve greater efficiency, by encouraging old farmers with small plots to sell out and retire. There was a large increase in trade with the West, to get Western technology. Certain big industrial enterprises were given more control over their production and planning, and were allowed to make overseas deals without government permission. Between 1971 and 1975 the national income rose by about 60% and industrial production by over 70%. Living standards rose; over a million new flats were built, and welfare benefits, such as old age pensions, improved. More goods were available in the shops, though supplies were erratic. Queues to buy meat sometimes started at midnight, and in 1975 frustrated housewives set fire to a Warsaw shop. Certain basic problems remained. Food subsidies took too much government money and food prices were too low, adding to the problem of shortages, but attempts to raise prices in 1976 by up to 60% led to widespread strikes. Poland owed vast sums of money in the West. By 1981 it took more than three-quarters of Poland's export trade just to finance the payment of the interest due.

Government control over the arts was relaxed by Gierek. Foreign plays and films were shown, and an underground press operated with minimal government interference. But the government was careful; outspoken critics were imprisoned. Church–State relations improved and more churches were opened. There was great excitement when the Polish Cardinal Wojtyla became Pope, and returned in 1979 as Pope John Paul II to pay a visit to his homeland.

1980 — strikes in the ports

But the economic problems remained intractable. In July 1980 Gierek tried yet again to raise the price of meat. The Polish workers reacted by a series of massive strikes and protests, centred on the traditionally militant northern ports of Gdansk and Szczecin. Although wage rises and a freeze on meat prices were conceded, the workers refused to go back until wider demands were met. Faced with ever-increasing strikes throughout the country, the government eventually gave way and signed a series of agreements in different industries. The most important points yielded were the rights of workers to strike and to form their own trade union movement, free from the control of the Communist Party. These were remarkable concessions by an eastern bloc government. The workers also gained greater access to the media for themselves and for the Roman Catholic Church, of which many were devout members. As the new independent trade union movement (which became known as 'Solidarity') rapidly gained members the

'Solidarity'

official trade unions were disbanded. By the middle of 1981 Solidarity had 10 million members and its leader, Lech Walesa, had become a figure of major national importance and of international fame. It seemed incredible that a mass movement of considerable unity and therefore strength should have emerged in a country where previously so little opportunity for it had apparently existed.

A Solidarity press conference, 1981

Gierek replaced   The initial crisis and the waves of unrest that followed brought changes in
by Kania   the governing group: ministers came and went at a rapid rate. In September
1980 Edward Gierek was replaced as First Secretary of the Communist
party by Stanislas Kania, and there were soon moves to unseat him in turn;
in February 1981 the Defence Minister General Jaruzelski became the
fourth Prime Minister within just over 12 months. The more liberal party
members made their weight felt. For the first time delegates to a party
Congress and the 200 Central Committee were elected by secret ballot, and
many prominent hardliners lost their places. But the basic economic
problems grew worse as the troubles went on: industrial output fell and the
country went further into debt. Some outside help in the form of food and
loans came from both West and East. Both sides hoped to bring some
stability to the situation: the West so that recently-won freedoms be
maintained, the eastern bloc so that Communist Party rule be upheld, the
troubles soon settled and the unrest prevented from spreading beyond
Poland's borders. Overshadowing the entire Polish situation lay the danger
of a Soviet-led military intervention to restore full Communist authority.
Warsaw Pact manoeuvres and speeches in language similar to that used
before the invasion of Czechoslovakia in 1968 threatened the Poles. On the
other hand the Soviet leaders also said that the Poles should be left to settle
their own affairs. They were no doubt hoping that their rather two-faced
behaviour would help keep the situation within bounds. They probably
wished to avoid having to intervene, knowing that the Polish army was
almost certain to resist and that any hopes of reasonable relations with the
West would disappear instantly.

Yet industrial peace was not quickly restored as the workers used their new-found power to make sure that the government did not go back on its agreements, and also to win further concessions. The strike weapon was also effective in forcing out of office unpopular local government officials. Massive demonstrations were organized in protest at the shortage of basic foods, many of which (including meat, butter, sugar, rice and wheat) were rationed anyway.

Martial law
imposedThe government continued a dialogue with Solidarity until the end of 1981. Lech Walesa was threatening strike action if the government went ahead with a special powers law, which included ending the right to strike. At the same time he was trying to curb other Solidarity leaders who felt that he was being too conciliatory towards the government and thought the time had come to challenge the Communist Party dictatorship. In December General Jaruzelski imposed martial law (military rule). Thousands of Solidarity members were arrested, including Lech Walesa. Basic civil rights, including freedom of speech, assembly, and travel were suspended and strict press censorship imposed. Strikes were banned. General Jaruzelski claimed that martial law was a temporary necessity until industrial peace had been restored and some of the economic problems solved. He promised that the changes of the last 18 months would not all be reversed, but warned that there could be no place for 'Solidarity extremists' who wanted the movement to challenge the power of the Communist Party.

Because of the news black-out confused reports emerged of resistance to the imposition of martial law, especially in the northern ports and the coal mines of Silesia. The government admitted some 5000 arrests and a few casualties. It preferred to emphasize how life was returning to normal, and how the Polish people had breathed a sigh of relief when the authorities had stepped in to halt the mounting chaos. The real situation remained unclear. In January 1982 the government announced massive food and fuel price increases, but whether martial law could bring effective solutions to the underlying economic problems remained to be seen. To a lesser extent the position of the Communist Party remained uncertain too. Its evident unpopularity had been revealed in the events since August 1980 and the resignation of half its members in the 18 months since that time. It had now been replaced as ruler by the army, albeit led by the Communist Party leader and Communist generals, and in the autumn of 1982 Solidarity was declared illegal.

(4) Hungary

Admiral Horthy had been deposed by the Germans in 1944 when he tried to take Hungary out of the war. His replacement survived only as long as German rule in eastern Europe. As Russian troops entered Budapest in 1945 they brought with them a newly appointed government led by Matyas Rakosi, a Jewish Communist, who had helped Bela Kun's Hungarian Soviet in 1919 and had later emerged as leader of the Hungarian Communists. The government was broadly based with three non-communist parties, but the presence of the Red Army and the Communist control of the secret police
'Salami tactics'*AVO* were used to undermine and destroy its opponents. Rakosi coined the phrase 'salami tactics', by which opposition was gradually sliced away like

pieces of sausage. The more conservative elements were accused of counter-revolutionary plots, while the more left wing were forced to merge with the Communists. The elections of 1947 were rigged, giving a Communist victory, and a new constitution and one-party state were introduced.

The familiar economic programme followed. Large-scale industry and trade were nationalized and collectivization in agriculture was forced on an unwilling peasantry. A great Hungarian industrial expansion, concentrating on iron, steel, and power, was launched. Great strides were made, but at the cost of the living standards of the average worker. Consumer goods and food were in short supply and hours of work were extremely long. All religious institutions were under attack and the head of the Roman Catholic Church in Hungary, Cardinal Mindszenty, was sentenced to life imprisonment in 1949 for plotting with the USA. As elsewhere in eastern Europe the 'Titoists' were rounded up on Stalin's orders in 1949. Anyone with Western connections was likely to be arrested, accused of dreadful crimes, and then sentenced to long terms of imprisonment or executed. At the time of the Russian 'Doctors Plot' a Zionist conspiracy was 'uncovered' in Hungary too. Rakosi had become like a 'little Stalin'. In 1953, on Stalin's death, he was ordered by Moscow to broaden his government and include Imre Nagy as Premier. The latter had been previously removed after a 'confession of guilt' in a Stalinist purge. The government admitted its previous mistakes and Nagy now promised a slackening of pace in the economy, with more consumer goods and food and less bullying of the workers and peasants. The previous trials were blamed on the Chief of Police and many political prisoners were freed. Hopes for more freedom grew, but seemed to be dashed when Rakosi and the hardliners removed Nagy from the premiership on the fall of Malenkov in Moscow.

Toppling Stalin's statue, Budapest 1956

1956 Revolt But hopes had been raised and the writers and students began to express their views more outspokenly than they had previously dared. They were encouraged in their mood by Khrushchev's 20th Party Congress speech in 1956, which revealed Stalin to have been a tyrant, and also by the concessions the Russians had just been forced to make in Poland (p. 126). Huge demonstrations took place and the crowds demanded 'Imre Nagy to the government' and 'Russians go home'. Rakosi was forced to resign and in October 1956 Nagy once again became Premier. Many soldiers joined those calling for change and gave weapons to newly established revolutionary councils. Barricades were built in the streets and the town of Debrecen in eastern Hungary was taken over. The mood of the people was such that the Russians seemed prepared to grant a certain measure of independence and to co-operate with a less harsh regime. Meanwhile, Nagy was being pushed further by the demands of the Hungarian people. He agreed to end one-party rule and to have a multi-party democracy with free elections. In November he announced Hungary's withdrawal from the Warsaw Pact. This was more than the Russian leaders could tolerate and plans to crush Hungary were put

Russian into effect. Taking advantage of the West's pre-occupation with the Suez
invasion crisis, Russian tanks occupied Budapest and, although many Hungarians fought the invaders, the result was never in doubt. Probably 3000 people died and anything up to 12 000 were arrested. Over 200 000 fled to the West. Nagy and others took refuge in the Yugoslav embassy and later gave themselves up on a promise of safety. They were promptly arrested, and executed in 1958.

Kadar's The government of Janos Kadar, which followed the 'October Revolu-
Hungary tion', did not completely return to the pre-1956 days, though there was an initial period of repression. Gradually, the atmosphere became far less rigid and the tone was set by a statement of Kadar's in 1961: 'Those who are not against us are with us.' Promotions to high positions in businesses became possible for non-party members; persecution of the Church ceased and the state started to help with its running costs. Greater freedom was allowed to writers, and western literature, plays and films were allowed. From 1971 voters were given something of a choice of Communist candidates at elections, though most were returned unopposed.

The year 1956 had shown the limits to which Hungary would be allowed to develop independently, but Kadar's government did offer the Hungarians increasing prosperity. To achieve this he was prepared to make moves away from the Soviet-style economy. Small-scale private workshops and services were encouraged and, in the public sector, higher incomes were offered as an incentive to greater output. Farmers were now given a fixed share of the profits on the collectives, so that if they did well their income rose. Their private plots were also increased in size.

The New This trend was further developed with the introduction in 1968 of the
Economic New Economic Mechanism. This lessened central government control over
Mechanism planning, allowed greater freedom for individual business initiative and reintroduced the idea of profitability, rather than simply supplying a demand laid down by the government. Individual factories were allowed to make their own trade agreements with the Western world and Western firms were encouraged to invest and build factories. The first to do so was the

West German metal corporation of Krupp. Prices of essentials remained controlled by a central commission; others were allowed to find their own level within limits, according to the demands of the market. Wage levels were also affected by the new policy. A top-level manager could get an 80% bonus if his firm made high profits. All these measures helped to stimulate growth in the economy and expansion was impressive. There was a 40% growth in output between 1971 and 1975 with the newer chemical and engineering industries doing well too. A lack of overall planning became evident, and to put this right a new state planning committee was established in 1973; yet strict central control was not reintroduced. Since then the economic growth rate has slowed considerably, but Hungary remains fairly prosperous and is the freest of the eastern bloc states.

(5) Romania

As in other countries occupied by the Red Army the Romanian Communist Party, which was tiny, initially collaborated with other political groups. The monarchy and Parliament continued, but opposition to the Communists was reduced by arrests of 'war criminals' and political opponents. Communists were placed in key positions in national and local government. A certain popularity was gained by distributing confiscated land. In 1947 the king, Michael, was forced to abdicate. A new constitution was introduced in 1948, which effectively made Romania a one-party state, and by 1952 all non-Communists had been removed from office. The new leader was Gheorghe Gheorghui-Dej, who established a strict, almost Stalinist, regime.

Establishment of one-party state

Romania had had very little industry before the Second World War and so the government embarked on a vast expansion of heavy industry. Thanks to large investments, deposits of petrol and other raw materials, and a plentiful supply of labour, progress was rapid. Agriculture did less well. A policy of collectivization was introduced, which was not very popular, although it allowed the peasants greater freedom than in other eastern bloc countries. However, agricultural output did increase: Romania remained self-sufficient in grain and even, at times, able to export.

Industrial expansion

The country was initially dominated by Russia, whose troops remained until 1957. As Romania had fought most of the war on the Nazi side huge reparations had to be paid, and all the property of foreign companies, mainly German and Italian, was taken over by the Russians. It was only under Khrushchev that reparations were stopped; Romanian property, with the exception of the uranium mines, handed back. Until the late 1950s Romania was very submissive to the Soviet Union, but from then on she began to assert her independence. In 1961 Khrushchev put forward proposals for the members of *Comecon* to integrate their economies, with each specializing in what they were best at. Romania was seen mainly as a supplier of raw materials and food for her more advanced neighbours. The Romanians, however, had other ideas. Their industry had been expanding at a rate of about 10% a year, admittedly from small beginnings, and they now planned further rapid growth with huge new steel works, an expanded chemical industry, and new enterprises, like the manufacture of oil installations. Her

Greater independence from Moscow

Parade in Romania in 1969

leaders therefore blocked the Russian plans in 1963 and did so successfully, for Khrushchev was concerned not to cause another split in the Communist camp while the rift with China and Albania was already there; and he was also still smarting from his climbdown over the Cuban missiles. Moreover, Romania could not easily be brought to heel because she had her own food and raw materials, including oil.

Independent foreign policy   Having established their own national line the Romanians soon showed their independence from the USSR in foreign policy. Diplomatic relations were resumed with Albania in 1963, and an economic mission was sent to the USA. Romania also refused to take sides in Russia's quarrel with China and increased her trade with the latter while other eastern bloc countries were doing the reverse. Trade with the capitalist world grew too, and many Western companies made agreements to build and operate factories and mills employing very recent technology.

Dej died in 1965 and was succeeded by Nicolae Ceasescu, one of his followers, who continued similar policies. In 1967 he went against eastern bloc policy by recognizing the West German government; the next year he condemned the Russian-led invasion of Czechoslovakia; and in 1972 he even welcomed the Israeli Prime Minister, Mrs Golda Meir, to Bucharest, while his Communist neighbours had no diplomatic relations with Israel. Although remaining within the Warsaw Pact Romania refused to allow its troops into the country for military exercises and would not put her troops under a joint command (i.e. in the charge of a Russian marshal). While the other Pact members were raising their military expenditure in the late 1970s, Romania refused to do so. Romanian foreign policy has maintained an independent line and Ceasescu has increasingly spoken up for the less developed world. He may well see himself as a possible successor to Tito as a leader of the non-aligned nations.

The rapid industrial expansion and assertion of a national line in economic and foreign policy proved popular with the Romanian people, although the rise in living standards has been limited by the concentration of investment in heavy industry, while agriculture has been neglected. Romanian oil was running dry by the late 1970s and this brought a problem, for the purchase of oil abroad meant a greater need to export and to attract foreign currency. One way of doing this was to encourage foreign tourists and over 3·5 million visited the country in 1977. But independence from Moscow has not meant a more liberal domestic policy. In fact, the regime Ceasescu's has been very strict, with a huge secret police force and little freedom for 'hard-line' individual expression. In 1979 Ceasescu called for artists 'to contribute to domestic policy enobling human personality, inspiring patriotism, devotion to socialism and happiness' and he said that religion was out of date in a scientific world. This is very Stalinist in its approach. So, too, is the huge personality cult which has been built up, glorifying Ceasescu himself.

(6) Bulgaria

Under King Boris Bulgaria had been a Nazi ally and this eventually led to defeat and to Russian occupation. In September 1944 a left-wing alliance, the Fatherland Front, in which the Communists played a substantial role, seized power with Russian support. The Communists used their positions Communist in the police and judiciary to get rid of the opposition and the people voted dictatorship to abolish the monarchy, under Boris' son Simeon, in 1946. In 1947 established a Communist dictatorship under the veteran Bulgarian Communist Dimitrov* was established. The country had strong ties with Russia, going back to the late 19th century when the Russians had helped the Bulgarians against the Turks. Soon Bulgaria became dominated by the Soviet Union. The leadership followed trends in Moscow very closely and at no time made any attempt to pursue an independent line. Traditional Communist policies were introduced. Collectives were enforced by 1960, and a programme of heavy industrialization was introduced. Starting from very small beginnings there was spectacular growth especially in metallurgy, engineering, and

---

*Dimitrov is also remembered because he was arrested in connection with the Reichstag Fire in Germany in 1933 (BWE, p. 39). The Soviet Union got him released and he became the head of *Comintern* between 1935 and 1943.

chemical fertilizer production. A country, which before the war had earned 75% of its money from agriculture, now earned 80% of its wealth from industry. Bulgaria has been a great supporter of *Comecon* and has received a large amount of financial support and loans from its bank. Tourism became a major money earner, too, with 4·5 million visitors in 1977. On the other hand, there has been little freedom of expression allowed to the Bulgarian people. The arts have been strictly censored and only works of 'socialist realism', glorifying communism, are supposed to be produced.

(7) Yugoslavia

Yugoslavia suffered partition and brutal treatment at the hands of the German forces who invaded the country in 1941. Further devastation was caused by the fighting between the two main resistance groups: the Chetniks, loyal to the monarchy, and the Partisans who were led by the Communist Josip Broz-Tito. It was the latter who liberated the country from the Germans without Russian help, and after the war Tito and the Yugoslav Communists remained in control; the Chetnik leader, Mihailovic, was executed. The pre-war monarchy was abolished and a Communist state was set up in 1946. The country was put on the usual Soviet course with industry nationalized and collective farms established. Yugoslavia had been very much an agricultural land; but she had a good supply of raw materials and industrialization soon led to growth in the iron and steel, and power

Tito and the Partisans

Marshal Tito and his staff

industries. Tito however, refused to become Stalin's lap-dog. Having been
The break with brought to power, not by the Red Army but by his own popularity, he was
Stalin successfully able to defy him. Stalin raged. Yugoslavia was expelled from
Cominform in 1948, and all economic aid from Russia was stopped. A
violent campaign was launched in all the eastern bloc countries against
Yugoslavia and Titoism. This failed to bring Tito down; in fact, it increased
his popularity at home, and Yugoslavia was soon adopting its own
independent line in home and foreign affairs.

Tito, perhaps with more confidence and imagination than some of his
eastern European counterparts, attempted to put socialism into practice
without using the rigid central control associated with the Communist bloc.
One sign of this was the setting up of elected 'workers' councils' which
'Workers' would give workers a say in the running of their companies. They were
councils' given powers over the organization of production, the use of investment, and
even the distribution of wages. In agriculture, the initial drive to collectivize
by force was halted, and most of the land returned to private ownership.
Compulsory deliveries to the state of farm produce were ended, and so were
restrictions on the buying and selling of land. However, a few state farms
and co-operatives did remain and the government had the 'socialization' of
agriculture as a long-term aim. Economic aid was sought and obtained in the
West.

New economic In the early 1960s many of the Communist economies showed signs of
policies stagnation and Yugoslavia was at the forefront of new economic policies,
which attempted to free the economy from tight central control without the
Communist party losing political control of the country. Prices of goods had
been fixed by the state and bore no relation to the amount available or the
demand for them.* Factories were not necessarily run to make a profit, but
simply to produce what the state wanted. From 1965 Tito and the more
liberal party members introduced far-reaching changes, which included
lifting all price control, insisting that all businesses make a profit or close,
and giving greater freedom to the individual factories. To start with, this led
to price increases and higher unemployment, but the economy adjusted
fairly rapidly and was soon expanding again. Many skilled workers went to
Germany and Austria where wages were far higher than at home. The
money they sent back to their families was very useful. Small private
businesses were encouraged as a means of solving some of the unemployment and also to provide services the government found it uneconomic to
run. Yugoslavia was opened up to foreign tourism on a large scale in the
1960s, and some 5·5 million visitors were going there annually by the late
1970s, bringing valuable foreign currency earnings. Many people set up
restaurants and other services for this increasing number of tourists. Contact
with the West was expanded in the business world too. Financial aid —
especially from the United States and from the International Monetary
Fund — provided vital investment and Western companies, who set up
factories in Yugoslavia, were welcomed. Trade links with the EEC brought
advanced machinery and technology, though at the expense of a huge trade
deficit. In attempting to continue the development drive the economy ran

*This is how prices find their level in the capitalist world — if something is scarce then its price tends to rise,
and vice versa.

into difficulties, in common with other countries, capitalist as well as communist. In the late 1970s inflation ran at about 30% (it reached 50% in 1980, the highest rate in Europe) and there was unemployment at the rate of 15% of those employed in the public sector.

The problem of separatist movements   Tito and the Communists tried to solve the ever-present problem of the many national groups in the country by organizing Yugoslavia as a Federation of six republics and two self-governing provinces. The various constitutions issued since the war have officially given much authority to the separate areas, although real power remains in Belgrade, the capital of Serbia as well as the whole country. It has been difficult to give the different areas real power without watching the whole country fall apart. Separatist movements have been strongest in the northern areas of Croatia and Slovenia, the richest provinces, some of whose people do not wish to help the poorer areas in the south. There has also been trouble in the southern province of Kossovo, where most of the people are Albanian. Tito did not flinch from dealing harshly with any nationalist movements inside the state, but they remain one of the great threats to Yugoslavia's existence and independence, because discontent could be used by an outside power (especially the USSR).

Yugoslavia was the freest state in the eastern bloc after 1948, with little government interference in the arts. But there were limits as to how far writers could go, especially in the fields of politics and sociology. When Tito's friend and Vice-President, Djilas, called for greater freedom and criticized the leadership, he was expelled from the party and imprisoned. Freedom of worship was allowed, though not encouraged, and Yugoslavia was the first Communist state to exchange representatives with the Vatican in 1966.

Foreign policy   Yugoslavia is a Communist country and as such is a natural ally of the other eastern bloc states. Relations with the USSR reached rock bottom during Stalin's last years, but they were somewhat repaired by Khrushchev in 1955. Since then they have varied a great deal, but always the Yugoslavs have refused to give up their own independent line. Yugoslavia is not a member of the CMEA or the Warsaw Pact and she strongly criticized the Russian-led invasions of Czechoslovakia in 1968 and of Afghanistan in late 1979. Tito became a major leader of the non-aligned nations (those states mainly in the less developed world who are neither in the American or Russian camp). At the 1979 conference of these states in Havana, Cuba, he argued strongly against his host Fidel Castro, who was proposing a pro-Moscow line.

Death of Tito, 1980   In 1980 Tito died, a few days before his eighty-eighth birthday, and the world waited to see what would happen when the dominant personality of the past 35 years was no longer there. Initially at least Yugoslavia continued on the same path; Tito's long fatal illness had allowed a period of adjustment. He had wanted a collective leadership to follow him, and the proposal for annual rotation of the office of President was adopted.

Yugoslavia remains of greater interest than its size might suggest that it warrants. It has shown the ability to preserve its independence within the Communist world and to develop its own form of socialism. This has given hope to many who have despaired at the brutality and strait-jacketing of other eastern European Communist regimes.

(8) Albania

Small mountainous Albania*, with its tribal traditions, shares a border with Yugoslavia. As in that country, a Communist regime came to power without any real Soviet support after a long resistance struggle against the Germans and Italians. A 'People's Republic' was declared in Albania in 1946 and has since been dominated by its former partisan leader, Enver Hoxha. Albania is the least developed country in eastern Europe and its Communist rulers

Modernization have begun the task of modernization. A pre-war illiteracy rate of 80% was by 1956 reduced to nil in the population under 40 years old, and certain basic industries, such as petrol, coal, and cement production, have been developed. The economy is run on Five-Year Plans and is state-controlled. Agriculture was forcibly collectivized but with limited results. The attitude of the leaders has remained hard-line Stalinist. Albania has the dubious

The first atheist distinction of having closed all its mosques and churches in 1966; it
state subsequently declared itself the first atheist state in the world.

Albania has always feared being swallowed up by Yugoslavia, which has a sizeable Albanian minority across the frontier. Its leaders feared that, as

The break with Khrushchev improved relations with Tito, Albania would be sacrificed,
Moscow; Hoxha turned to China for protection and tried to play Moscow off against
friendship with Peking to safeguard the country's existence. When the Russians tried to
China bring him to heel, Hoxha had the nerve to go to Moscow and attack Russian domestic and foreign policy as weak. Khrushchev then broke off diplomatic relations in 1961, and Albania moved totally into the Chinese 'camp', receiving substantial financial aid. In 1968 Hoxha condemned the Russian-led invasion of Czechoslovakia in harsh terms and withdrew Albania from the Warsaw Pact. Disenchantment with China grew in the 1970s as the latter's relations with the USA were improved, and Hoxha criticized the new Chinese leaders when Mao died. In June 1978 Albania supported Vietnam in her quarrel with China and, as a result, all Chinese aid was stopped. Albania therefore began to look to Greece, Turkey, and even the EEC to increase trade.

(9) Czechoslovakia

Democracy President Benes returned to Prague in 1945 to head a coalition government
restored in which the Communists played a substantial part, thanks to a short-lived Russian military presence and to the party's popularity. Communists received 38% of the vote in free elections held in 1946 and were the largest single party. At first it looked as though the Czech tradition of democracy would continue. Benes, however, did not have a completely free hand, for the Russians forced the Czechs to refuse Marshall Aid from America, which

1948 The they had wanted to accept. At home, the Czech Communists used their key
Communist positions in the army and police to slice away at their opponents. In 1948 the
'coup' non-Communist government ministers resigned in protest at the way the

*Not much bigger than Wales, which has nearly twice the population.

Communists had packed the police with their supporters. Immense pressure was brought to bear on Benes — a sick man — by the Communists inside the country, and by threatening Russian troop movements outside. Jan Masaryk, the non-Communist Foreign Minister and son of the inter-war president, was found dead, having fallen from a window at the Foreign Office. It is still unclear whether it was murder, suicide, or accident. Benes soon resigned and died the same year (1948). Czechoslovakia became a Communist dictatorship with Klement Gottwald as its leader.

Because Czechoslovakia was a highly developed society with a tradition of freedom* it did not bend easily to the Soviet model, and a wholesale regimentation was enforced. Well over 100 000 people were locked up and great public show trials, similar to those in Moscow in the 1930s, were staged. Many of those actually executed were Jewish, which fitted in well with Stalin's policy of discovering 'Zionist' enemies. Gottwald died in 1953 (having caught pneumonia at Stalin's funeral) and the leadership of the party fell to Antonin Novotny, a hard-liner, who was to show remarkable skill in keeping himself in power. Under his rule there was very little de-Stalinization after 1956, no admission of 'past errors', as elsewhere in the Communist world, and no real relaxation.

With its highly developed industries, especially those in metals and armaments, Czechoslovakia was a very valuable member of the Soviet bloc. The nationalization of industry started under Benes and followed easily from the German war-time control. It was continued after 1948 and expansion was pushed ahead. Some areas did well; Slovakia, for example, became a mixed agricultural/industrial area with steel works and a chemical industry.

Economic problems As a whole, the economy was stretched beyond all reasonable limits, and it was made to concentrate almost solely on heavy industry for the benefit of the Soviet Union. By the mid 1960s Russia was taking about 40% of Czechoslovakia's total foreign trade. Despite being forced to sell cheaply to the USSR she made a good profit on her trade, but this was 'frozen' in Russia and used to build up Russian industry. The Czech people suffered as a result. They had low incomes, a lack of goods to buy, few services and a chronic housing shortage. There was a very high rate of abortion to prevent the birth of unwanted children: some 800 000 legal abortions between 1959 and 1968, in a population of something over 14 million. The drafting of people into industry, plus a policy of forced collectivization without much financial investment, caused disasters in agriculture too. From having had enough food to feed her population Czechoslovakia became an importer of huge quantities of meat and wheat. By the early 1960s the growth rate in the whole economy had dropped to nothing. It was not possible to stifle all criticism and increasing numbers inside the party and in the leadership itself were appalled at the economic situation.

'Socialism with a human face' 1968 Novotny was finally forced out in January 1968 and was replaced as First Secretary by Alexander Dubcek, the Slovak Communist party leader. It soon became apparent that the new leadership, which included Svoboda as President and Cernik as Prime Minister, would not simply blame the deposed leaders for past mistakes, utter a few promises, and then carry on as

---

* Exactly 100 years before, liberal revolutionaries in Prague had been bombarded into silence by the Habsburg General Windischgrätz.

before. They began to introduce 'socialism with a human face' which promised freedom of speech and the press, and a greater say for the people in how the country was run. Dubcek talked of allowing some freedom to political parties opposed to the Communists, and of permitting the economy to be run free of party control. This revival of the democratic traditions buried for 20 years deeply shocked the Russians and the hard-liners in the eastern bloc. The East German press was the most forthright in its attack, claiming that the 'enemies of the party' and 'the servants of imperialism' had achieved power, and that honest Communists were committing suicide in despair. Dubcek tried hard to convince the Russian leaders that the government was in control of events; that the Czechs had no intention of leaving the eastern bloc or the Warsaw Pact; and that they simply wished to pursue a line of development suitable to their own society and economy.

Russian troops enter Prague   For a while the Russians waited on events. They warned the Czech leaders not to go too far, they held Warsaw Pact military exercises on Czech soil as a threat, and they tried to split the united front of the leadership. Having failed to alter events to suit themselves Russian-led forces invaded Czechoslovakia on 21 August 1968. Prague was quickly occupied. Armed resistance would have been useless. The Czech leaders tried to salvage something from the 'Prague Spring' to avoid a complete return to the pre-1968 situation. Initially the Russians allowed the leadership to remain in power, but insisted they silence any criticism in the press and media. In 1969 there were riots following jubilation at a Czech ice-hockey victory over the Russians, and Dubcek was dismissed as First Secretary. He was sent as ambassador to Constantinople, but was soon recalled. He was expelled from the party and given a menial job in a Czech woodyard. His replacement was Gustav

Husak's Czechoslovakia   Husak, who had been a victim of Stalinism and therefore had a good public image. Husak presided over a thorough purge of the party at all levels, and saw that critics of the Russian invasion of 1968 were removed from all teaching, judicial, police, and managerial posts. The press was once more made the voice of the Soviet view and was soon declaring that the Russians had secured 'freedom and socialism' in Czechoslovakia by their prompt action; they had saved the country from the Zionist plot of a 'clique of Jewish

Change in Czechoslovakia

intellectuals'. The 1970s witnessed no relaxation; and dissidents, people who do not follow official government views, were continually harassed by the police. The most outspoken critics, such as those who established the Charter 77 movement to try to safeguard human rights and freedom of expression as laid down by the 1975 Helsinki agreement (CORE, p. 161), were tried for subversion and anti-state activities and imprisoned. The authorities took an increasingly harsh line with critics of the regime as the 1970s progressed, because the economy got into serious difficulties again. The price of basic necessities went up considerably in 1979, especially fuel because of its shortage. Heating oil, for example, went up suddenly by 125%. Economic problems can easily lead to political discontent and the pro-Russian government was not prepared to take any chances.

Glossary

Anti-Semitism	Anti-Jewish racial prejudice
Bourgeois	Middle-class; used by Marxists in a condemnatory manner
Capitalism	System in which properties and businesses are owned privately by individuals or companies
De-Stalinization	Process by which the worst features of Stalin's dictatorship were removed
Dissident	Person speaking out against a prevailing system; usually criticizing a government in a country where this is forbidden
Eastern bloc	The East European Communist countries
Euro-communism	The policy of those western European Communist parties which refuse to follow Moscow's line
Indemnity (or **Reparations**)	Money paid by the loser in a war to the victor
Intelligentsia	Highly educated intellectuals, e.g. professors
Left or **left-wing** **Right** or **right-wing**	Political terms denoting attitudes. 'Left' usually means willingness to change, some times drastically, the structure of politics and society; 'right' a general hostility to change and a wish to preserve the existing structure. The left generally favours sharing the wealth of the country; the right, free enterprise and capitalism. Communism is an extreme form of left-wing politics, Fascism of right-wing.
Lend-Lease	Wartime (1941–5) arrangement whereby the USA supplied materials to Britain and Russia
Nationalization (without compensation)	Government takeover of property (without paying the previous owner)
Ostpolitik	Policy promoted by West German Chancellor Willi Brandt in late 1960s which recognized the division of Germany and tried to lessen tension by agreements with the Communist eastern bloc

Peaceful Coexistence	Willingness of different systems, communism and capitalism, to live in peace, recognising each other's right to exist
Peoples's Democracy or **Republic**	Usual official title of a Communist country
Purge	The cleaning-up of a party or organization, involving the expulsion of members not considered fit to belong
Reparations	See **Indemnity**
Satellite state	A small state dependent on or controlled by a great power; term used to describe the east European countries in relation to the USSR
Socialism	According to Karl Marx a first stage on the road to Communism
Stalinist	Term used to describe any system similar to the Soviet Union under Stalin's regime
Third World	The poorer, less developed areas of the world, uncommitted to either capitalism or communism in the Cold War rivalry
Titoists	Term used in late 1940s and early 1950s to indicate those who, like President Tito, declined to follow the policies of Stalin
Zionist	A supporter of the Jewish state of Israel; often used by Communists to mean 'imperialist' or to provide a cloak for crude anti-Semitism

Booklist

Jackson N.C., *Russia in the Twentieth Century* (Wheaton, 1978, 130pp): a straightforward narrative account of Russia's history from 1900 to the early 1970s

Quinn, J., *The Russian Revolution* (University Tutorial Press, 1978, 52pp): a study of the main features of the Russian Revolution

Mack, W., *Lenin and the Russian Revolution* (Longman, 1970, 104pp); Cubitt, H., *Russia under the Last Tsar* (Longman 1980, 96pp): Mack and Cubitt are in the usual 'Then and There' format and cover the same area with different emphasis — the former concentrates on the years of revolution, the latter on the whole reign of Nicholas 11 and the general features of early 20th century Russia

Hartley, L., *The Russian Revolution* (Evans Bros., 1980, 48pp): a general introduction with the events of 1914–1921 in some detail; a double-page format for each chapter with questions to answer

Robottom, J., *Modern Russia* (Longman, 1972, 170pp): a general narrative account with a concentration on events to Stalin's death in 1953

Gibson, M., *Tito* (Wayland, 1981, 72pp): a survey of the life of the Yugoslav partisan and Communist leader till his death; includes a number of photos *

2 filmstrip/cassette presentations by E.A.V. Ltd. are useful: *The Russian Revolution* deals with the background to the revolution of 1917 and events to Lenin's death in 1924; *The Soviet Union; Half a Century* is a more general study — both use a wide range of photographs, artwork, and charts.

The following books are recommended for further reading:

Grey, I., *The First Fifty Years* (Hodder & Stoughton, 1976, 558pp): a detailed account of the collapse of the Tsarist regime, and Soviet Russia 1917–1967 *

Nove, A., *Stalinism and After* (George Allen and Unwin, 1975, 208pp): a study of the Stalinist regime in Russia, how it came about and how far the Stalinist system has been modified since Stalin's death

Nove, A., *An Economic History of the USSR* (Pelican, 1978, 416pp): a thorough account of the Soviet economy centred on the years 1917–1964; it includes many statistical charts

Kochan, L., *The Making of Modern Russia* (Penguin, 1970, 336pp): a history of Russia to 1953; about 100pp on the years since 1905

Deutscher, I., *Stalin: A Political Biography* (Pelican, 1974, 682pp): the standard biography of Stalin with analysis of his rule *

Summers, A. and Mangold, T., *The File on the Tsar* (Fontana, 1977, 416pp): a book that takes the whole mystery surrounding the 'execution' of the Russian royal family in 1918 and suggests that the traditional view that the whole family was killed is faulty

Nettl, J.P., *The Soviet Achievement* (Thames and Hudson, 1967, 288pp): a general history of Communist Russia to 1964 with less emphasis on the personalities involved than in most books; very interesting pictures and artwork included

McAuley, M., *Politics and the Soviet Union* (Penguin, 1977, 352pp): an explanation of the major changes in Russia from the revolution to the Khrushchev years; emphasis on explaining the adoption of policies

Salisbury, H.E., *Russia in Revolution 1900-1930* (A. Deutsch, 1978, 288pp): a fascinating collection of photos and artwork of the first 30 years of this century

Kaiser, R., *Russia; the People and the Power* (Pelican, 1976, 469pp): a personal view of everyday life in Russia by a man who worked there for a number of years and who interviewed a number of Russian emigrés

Staar, R.E., *The Communist Regimes in Eastern Europe* (Hoover Institution Publications, 1977, 297pp): a study of the individual countries plus the moves to political, economic, and military integration*

Polonsky, A., *The Little Dictators* (Routledge and Kegan Paul, 1975, 224pp): a study of the states of Eastern Europe from their emergence as independent countries to World War Two; it emphasises social and economic problems, political developments, and the treatment of minorities; an epilogue suggests the trends of development from the war to the 1970s

Fejtö, F., *A History of the People's Democracies* (Pelican, 1974, 560pp): Eastern Europe from the Stalinist days to the early 1970s; it includes the effects of Russian domination as well as the individual developments within the eastern bloc

Wilson, D., *Tito's Yugoslavia* (Cambridge Univ. Press, 1980, 269pp): Yugoslavia 1945-mid 1970s; it looks at the unique brand of communism developed by Tito and his international role.

Rothschild, J., *East Central Europe Between the Two World Wars* (Univ. of Washington Press 1975, 480pp): an advanced study of the area including developments in each country; its sequel is *East Central Europe Since 1939* by W. S. Vucinich

Purnell's History of the Twentieth Century: 10 volumes published in 1972 with articles by various authors; many of the events including some less obvious aspects of the history of the 20th century are included; each volume includes very interesting artwork and photos which give the events real impact

Some novels which could prove interesting:
Solzhenitsyn, A., *One day in the life of Ivan Denisovitch*; *The First Circle*; *Gulag Archipelago*: these all deal with the prison camps of Russia

Sholokhov, M., *And Quiet Flows the Don* and *The Don Flows Home to the Sea* are stories of the Cossacks during the years of the First World War and Revolutions. *Virgin Soil Upturned* and *Harvest on the Don* deal with the years of collectivization

*Every effort has been made to check that publication details given here are correct. Some books referred to appear to have gone out of print — these are indicated by an asterisk (*). Despite this, these books have been included, as the authors feel they are very useful and relevant, and it should be possible to obtain copies from libraries.

Index

Readers should also refer to the table of contents.

Afghanistan 112, 115, 117, 137
agriculture in Russia, early 20th century 1; (1918) 21, 32-3; NEP 33-5; end of NEP 45-7; first Five-Year Plans 49-51; (1945-) 93, 95; (1955-) 101-3; (1964-) 111-12
Albania 109, 119-23
Andropov, Yuri, 118n
April Theses 16-17
arts, the, in Russia 55-6, 94, 98, 113-14
atom bomb 89, 91

Battles:
  Kursk (1943) 69
  Masurian Lakes (1914) 12
  Stalingrad (1942-3) 68-9
  Tannenberg (1914) 12
  Tsushima Straits (1905) 8
Benes, Edouard 87, 88, 138-9
Beria, Lavrentii 58, 97-8, 99
Berlin 89, 92, 106, 107, 115, 124
Bloody Sunday (1905) 8
Bolsheviks, the 8, 15, 16-23
Brezhnev, Leonid 110-17
Britain 28-32, 37, 61, 87
Bukharin, Nikolai 45, 47, 57, 100
Bulgaria 62, 71, 72-7, 91, 108, 119-23

Castro, Fidel 107, 137
Ceasescu, Nicolae 133-4
Cheka 24, 29, 32, 33
China 61, 62, 92, 107-9, 115-6
Church, the 4, 24, 98, 114, 123, 125-6, 127, 130, 138
Churchill, Winston 32, 65, 70, 71, 89, 91
collective farms 47, 49-51, 59-60, 68, 93, 103, 119, 124, 126, 130, 132, 134, 138, 139
'Cold War', the 88-92, 105, 113, 114
Comecon (the CMEA) 91, 121, 122, 132, 135, 137

Cominform 91, 92, 121, 122, 136
Comintern 37, 62, 71
Communism, early ideas, see Marx
Constituent Assembly, the 24-5
Constitution, the (1924) 35-7; (1936) 59; (1977) 118
Cuba 107, 109, 137
Curzon Line 78
Czechoslovakia 30-1, 62-3, 69, 72-7, 88-91, 108; (invasion, 1968) 115, 117, 122, 134, 137, 138, 139-40

Danzig 63, 78, 80 (see also Gdansk)
Détente 114
'Dictatorship of the Proletariat' 6, 23
Doctors' Plot (1952) 94, 97, 100, 121, 130
Dubcek, Alexander 139-40
Dumas, the 11, 14

education 54-5, 105, 123
Estonia 27, 64, 72, 77-8
Eurocommunism 117

famine (1921) 35; (1933) 50, 52
Five Year Plans (1928-41) 45-53; (1946-51) 93; (1952-) 103; (1956-) 103; (1981-5) 112
France 28-32, 62, 87, 92

Gagarin, Yuri 104
Gdansk 126-7
Germany 12-20, 27, 37, 38, 61-70, 77, 79, 80, 81, 83, 85, 87-8, 89
German Democratic Republic (GDR) 92, 107, 115, 122, 140
Gierek, Edward 127-8
Gomulka, Wladislaw 125-6
Gottwald, Klement 139
Greece 71, 91

Helsinki Agreement (1975) 114, 115, 141

Horthy, Admiral 80, 129
'Hot Line', the (1963) 107
Hungary 37, 69–71, 72–7, 89, 91, 116, 119–23; 1956 Revolution 101, 108, 122, 131
Husak, Gustav 140

'Iron Curtain' 91
Iron Guard (Romania) 83

Japan 8, 28–32, 62, 64, 71
Jaruzelski, General 128–9
Jews 4, 68, 79, 81, 82, 94, 98, 114, 121, 125, 139, 141
John Paul II, Pope 127
July Days, the 17

Kadar, Janos 123, 131
Kamenev, Lev 44–5, 57
Kennedy, President J. F. 106–7
Kerensky, Alexander 17–22
Khrushchev, Nikita 58, 97–109, 112
KGB 113
Kirov, Sergei 56
Kolkhoz, *see* Collective Farms
Konsomol 55
Korea 88–9, 105–6
Kornilov, General 19, 20, 22
Kosygin, Alexei 110–17
Kronstadt 17, 34, 36
Kulaks 35, 45–6, 49–50, 60
Kun, Bela 80, 129

Land Law, the (1917) 23
Latvia 27, 64, 72, 77–8
League of Nations 38, 62, 64
Lend Lease 69–70
Lenin, Vladimir, early life 7–8; return to Russia 16–17; seizure of power 18–20; in power 23–38; political testament 38, 98; death and assessment 39
Leningrad 39, 68
Lithuania 27, 64, 72, 77–8, 114
Little Entente, the 80, 87
Litvinov, Maxim 61, 64
living standards 52, 104–5, 112, 117, 123

machine tractor stations (MTS) 51, 103
Malenkov, Georgi 58, 97–101
Mao Tse-tung 92, 108, 116
Marshall Aid 91, 121, 138
Marx, Karl 5–7, 15, 23, 34
Masaryk, Jan 139
Masaryk, Tomas 86–7

Memel 78
Mensheviks 8, 15, 18, 23, 27, 36
Molotov, Vyacheslav 64, 97
Moscow 27, 67
Munich Conference (1938) 63
Muslims 114

Nagy, Imre 130, 131
Narodniks 7 (*see also* Socialist Revolutionaries)
Nepmen 35
New Economic Policy (1921) 33–5, 37, 45–8
Nicholas II, Tsar 1–20; death 33
NKVD 57, 58
North Atlantic Treaty Organization (NATO) 92, 106

October Manifesto (1905) 11
OGPU 56
Olympic Games (1980) 114, 116
Operation Barbarossa 64
Order Number One (1917) 15, 21
'Ostpolitik' 115, 125

Pacts, *see* Treaties
Paris Summit (1960) 106
'Peaceful Co-existence' 106, 114
Pilsudski, Marshal Josef 31, 78–80
Poland 1, 13, 27, 31, 62–4, 66, 71, 72–7, 89, 91, 108, 119–23; (1956 troubles) 101, 108, 122, 126; (1980 troubles) 123, 127–9
Politburo 36
'Popular Fronts' 62
Potsdam Treaty (1945) 89, 124
Provisional Government (1917) 14–22
Purges (1930s) 56–8

Rakosi, Matyas 129–131
Red Guards, Red Army 20, 21, 29–32; *see also* sections on World War II
Romania 62, 64, 69, 71, 72–7, 89, 91, 108, 116, 119–23
Roosevelt, President F. D. 71, 89

'Scorched earth' policy 66
Secret Police in Russia, *see*, Cheka, OGPU, NKVD, KGB
'Secret Speech', the (1956) 98–100, 121
serfs 1
Seven Year Plan (1959) 103
'Show Trials' (1930s) 57–8
Social Democratic Party (Russia) 5
'Socialism in One Country' 44, 61
'Socialist Realism' 56, 94

Socialist Revolutionaries 7, 15, 18, 23, 24, 27, 31, 33
'Solidarity' 123, 127-9
Solzhenitsyn, Alexander 113-4
Soviets 9, 15, 20, 23, 24, 36
space travel 104, 113
Sputnik 104, 106
Stakhanov, Alexei 53
Stalin, Josef 23, 36, 38-9, 42-70; attacks on (1956) 98-100; image (1964-) 113
state farms 51, 112
Strategic Arms Limitation Talks (SALT) 115
Sudetenland 87

Teheran Conference (1943) 71
Tereshkova, Valentina 104
'Thaw', the 98
Tito, Josip Broz 91, 108, 121, 122, 123, 134, 135-7, 138
Transylvania 80, 82
Treaties:
  Brest-Litovsk (1918) 27, 37
  Helsinki (1975) 114, 115, 141
  Kellogg-Briand Pact (1928) 61
  NATO (1949) 92, 106
  Nazi-Soviet Pact (1939) 64, 80, 96
  Non-Proliferation (1968) 114
  Potsdam (1945) 89, 124
  Rapallo (1922) 38, 61, 62
  Riga (1921) 31
  Strategic Arms Limitation (SALT) (1972) 115
  Test Ban (1963) 107, 114
  Trianon, the (1920) 80, 81
  Warsaw Pact (1955) 106, 108
  Yalta (1945) 71, 89, 124, 125

Trotsky, Leon 9, 10, 20, 22, 23, 27, 29-32, 34, 38-9, 44, 47, 57-8, 100
Truman, President H. 89
Truman Doctrine (1947) 92
Turkey 27, 37, 91, 107

Ukraine, the 27, 35
Ulbricht, Walter 124
United Nations Organization (UNO) 71, 92, 106, 115, 125
United States of America (USA) 62, 70-1, 92, 112, 115, 116, 138

Vietnam 115
virgin lands scheme 102, 110

Walesa, Lech 127-9
War Communism 32-3
Wars:
  Civil (1918-21) 27-33, 91
  Finnish (1939-40) 64
  Spanish Civil (1936-9) 62
  World War I 12-14
  World War II 61-70
Warsaw Pact (1955) 106, 108, 115, 122, 131, 134, 137, 138, 140
Warsaw Rising 69
Wilson, President Woodrow 72, 78
writers in Russia 56, 98, 113-4

Yalta Conference and Treaty (1945) 71, 89, 124, 125
Yugoslavia 69, 71, 72-7, 91, 108, 121-2, 138

Zhdanov, Andrei 56, 94
Zhukov, Marshal 66, 100
Zinoviev, Gregory 37, 44-5, 57, 100